This book
purchase was
made possible by
a grant from the
California State
Library

CALIFORNIA
STATE LIBRARY

RETIREMENT REINVENTION

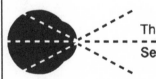

RETIREMENT REINVENTION

MAKE YOUR NEXT ACT YOUR BEST ACT

ROBIN RYAN

THORNDIKE PRESS

A part of Gale, a Cengage Company

GALE
A Cengage Company

Farmington Hills, Mich • San Francisco • New York • Waterville, Maine
Meriden, Conn • Mason, Ohio • Chicago

Thorndike Press® Large Print Lifestyles.
The text of this Large Print edition is unabridged.
Other aspects of the book may vary from the original edition.
Set in 16 pt. Plantin.

LIBRARY OF CONGRESS CIP DATA ON FILE.
CATALOGUING IN PUBLICATION FOR THIS BOOK
IS AVAILABLE FROM THE LIBRARY OF CONGRESS

ISBN-13: 978-1-4328-5354-9 (hardcover)

Published in 2018 by arrangement with Penguin Books, an imprint of Penguin Publishing Group, a division of Penguin Random House LLC

Printed in Mexico
1 2 3 4 5 6 7 22 21 20 19 18

FOR MY FAMILY:
Steve, Jack, and Mom

In loving memory of my father
Joseph "JC" Christiano,
1925–2017

CONTENTS

FOREWORD 9

PART 1. WHAT CAN MY FUTURE LOOK LIKE?

Chapter 1. Make a Plan: Don't Become a Failed Retiree!. 17

Chapter 2. What Do You Want to Do Now? 54

Chapter 3. Where to Live: New Home, Two Homes, Stay Put? 90

Chapter 4. $$$$$$: Dealing with Money Issues 113

Chapter 5. Overcoming Obstacles . . 137

Chapter 6. Transitioning 157

PART 2. WHAT YOU CAN DO

Chapter 7. We All Need Social Connection 183

Chapter 8. Making a Difference and Giving Back 200

Chapter 9. Live Your Hobby 258
Chapter 10. Travel 304
Chapter 11. Learn! Education and
    New Skills (Cheap or Free). . . 344
Chapter 12. Start a Business 354
Chapter 13. Live a Better Future . . 384

MORE CAREER HELP
   IS AVAILABLE 395
   ACKNOWLEDGMENTS 397

FOREWORD

I was scared. No, I was downright terrified. I couldn't feel anything. I couldn't even think about anything. I simply sat on that examination table waiting. Moments later the door handle turned and a coldhearted radiologist stood in the doorway and said, "Mrs. Ryan, you have breast cancer and you need a mastectomy." Those awful words that no woman ever wants to hear. And like every person who gets a cancer diagnosis, my world was shattered in seconds.

I would fight for my life for the next two years and, of course, close down my business. This book is a symbol of my recovery, and I want you to benefit from what I learned: *live for now.* You don't know what tomorrow will bring. Cancer is a terrifying experience. I went through four surgeries and extensive chemo. I was left with nerve pain so excruciating that I stayed on serious painkillers for nine months. That nerve

9

damage became permanent. Chemo is an awful experience — if you have never gone through it, I hope you never do. They literally are poisoning you, and you become so, so ill. It takes everything you've got to battle the cancer in your body. Some of us are blessed by God, and we win. Sadly, many people lose.

While I was sick, my friend and former secretary Wanda Bartel died from cancer at the age of fifty-three. I couldn't wrap my head around how this vibrant, expressive lady died. She just couldn't, but she did, and I was absolutely devastated. We also buried one of the hockey moms whose son played on my son's team. Jennifer Mc-Cutcheon and I were diagnosed with breast cancer one week apart, and this nice lady lost the battle. She was in her early fifties.

I survived. But living through something as scary and traumatic as cancer (and losing those ladies during that time) absolutely changes you. I don't look at the world the same way. I try to appreciate a little bit more each day. I love my family and cherish our moments together more dearly. I look at my son, Jack, and am ever so grateful I will see him go to college, graduate, marry someday, and maybe even give me a grandchild. I have so many more days I can spend with him. Although I do live with chronic pain, I always remind myself that both Wanda and Jennifer would have given anything to see their sons grow up.

I witnessed the good in people. I appreciated my caring friends for all they did to help me and just for being part of my supportive world. Kind friends drove me to doctors, physical therapy, and anywhere I needed to go. Strangers sent me cards, and thoughtful friends wrote me supportive notes. In the last year, I even forgave a good friend who walked away when I got sick. That was hard to do, but in forgiving her I found more peace. No, I haven't forgotten how she turned her back on me. Some situations end badly — I just accepted that as a challenging part of life.

It took me two years to recover and be able to start to work again, even part-time. I missed helping my clients land new jobs, but there were many days when I was pretty convinced that I could never do it again, never write again, never feel well enough to give a speech. Many people suffer from something called "chemo brain" or "chemo fog." You just can't think very clearly or remember much. You walk around in a fog. Boy, is it disheartening. And it takes a long, long time to clear up. I was blessed in being able to recover enough to write this book. My goal was to make a difference. I wanted to be able to help you and other baby boomers who might need some final-career-stage advice on more effective ways to plan *happy years* of retirement. So I dedicated myself to helping you.

Now, you also have to help yourself. It's up to you to create a plan that allows you to go forward and make your retirement a prime time of your life. Your best days are still ahead of you! Your very best day is today, because it may be all you're given. I want to encourage you to live your days to the fullest. Life will interrupt you. There will be tragedies in the days ahead, big losses of family and friends. There will be hard, challenging times. I can't take that from you.

Live for the good days. I encourage you to do the things on your bucket list as soon as possible. I want you to make a retirement plan that inspires you to get out there and start living it right now. Do the fun and meaningful things that make you truly happy, satisfied, and fulfilled.

As you continue living your life, take time to smell the roses. I notice the world around me more. The new life of spring, the sunny days of summer, the vibrant leaves of fall. I enjoy watching the ocean waves crash, hoping for big, powerful ones. I love walking in new snow that is pristine and white, where nature looks like a Christmas card. And I love flowers. I make time to photograph them and delight in their natural beauty. Flowers are exquisite creations of nature, but if you don't take time to look at how perfect they are, you're going to miss them — and a lot else, I'm afraid. Enjoying the beauty of nature should be part of how you enjoy leisure time.

This *is* the best time of your life, because this is *the* moment that you're living right now. Make each day memorable and worthwhile. Retirement is a great time of life if you develop and enact a worthwhile plan to make it so.

So now let's explore exactly how to make your retirement meaningful, fun, and enjoyable.

> P.S. All my book profits are donated to breast cancer research.

■ ■ ■ ■

PART 1:
WHAT CAN MY
FUTURE LOOK LIKE?

■ ■ ■ ■

Don't go through life — grow through life.

PART 1:
WHAT CAN MY
FUTURE LOOK LIKE?

Don't go through life — grow through life.

CHAPTER 1
MAKE A PLAN:
DON'T BECOME A
FAILED RETIREE!

Success is relishing life and doing
whatever will make you truly happy.

When you leave work, you will likely have
over 9,000 days to fill up. 9,000 days! How
will you spend them? What would make
those days meaningful and enjoyable? These
are the million-dollar questions you need to
answer.

Society sends people an awful message
once they hit retirement age: *your best days
are behind you.* People often fear retirement
because they see what they will lose or give
up, and not what they will gain. They may
fear too much freedom with no purpose.
Referred to by past generations as the
"golden years," this life stage was the end of
your work life, and left you with little to
dream about except travel and family. But
what about your identity? Your self-worth?
Your need to be productive and important

in your own eyes? What about your emotional well-being? Your creative soul? 9,000 days is a lot of time to fill only with leisure. Don't you still want a sense of purpose and of belonging to a community too?

Developing a meaningful and enjoyable retirement takes some work and planning. It doesn't just naturally happen. In fact, not enacting a good plan can put you on the road to becoming a "failed retiree." That's right, as you enter this next and final phase of your career, you might actually FAIL!

Financial planners all have war stories about people who retired and became absolutely miserable. Too much time off, and nothing worthwhile to do. Within one to two years, the retirees were hitting the pavement, looking to return to work, only to find no one was interested in hiring them. So in retirement they failed. Don't let this happen to you. To make your future a happy one, you need to do some self-exploration and examine your interests, values, and hobbies. Your future goals need to be shaped by who you are today and what you truly want. Leaving your working life behind does bring freedom from stress and the daily grind, but it can also leave you alone, with an awful lot of time on your hands.

The all-important question, then, is: *What*

is your life going to look like?

Careers give us purpose, identity, and meaning. For past generations, retirement involved leaving work behind. But it too often included sitting around and watching TV as a major life highlight. That plan has become old-fashioned. What if you reinvent the game and make up new rules for your retirement? What if you look ahead and say it's time to use an interest to start a new career — likely part-time — simply because you enjoy it? You could tap a current interest or find a cause you care about and use some time to give back and help others. This new career would be *fun* and fill a few hours each week with meaning while leaving plenty of time for other activities, socializing, and leisure.

Leaving behind the "professional me" gave Dick pause. He had been a chemistry teacher in a small town for over thirty-five years and had also served as the high school's assistant football and lacrosse coach. He knew all the kids and families in the area — in some cases going back generations — and was well-liked in the community. But living in a small, rural town, his options for Retirement Reinvention were limited. While he was definitely tired of grading papers and working long hours, he loved his job and worried a lot about what he'd be losing: he was concerned that he would no longer feel connected or that he did something important. But when New York State offered incentives to older and more expensive teachers to retire, Dick decided to take the package.

It was an ad for a Meals on Wheels driver that got his attention. "That three-day-a-week job didn't sound exciting: delivering meals to elderly people and shut-ins. But it left lots of time for golfing and being with my two young grandsons," Dick remembers. "The most important thing, of course, was that I would be helping people."

It turned out that this was a perfect fit for Dick. "I greeted each person by name and stayed to chat for a few minutes, knowing that the elderly were often pretty isolated, especially during the cold, snowy winter months. It turned out that many of their kids were my former students, so I'd remind them of the connection, which gave us an instant bond. I always asked if I could do something extra — take out the trash or change a lightbulb in the ceiling," he says.

At first, many of the people he delivered to were not open to his efforts: they were elderly, frail, and often grumpy. Yet he always arrived with a smile, because he knew the work he did was important. And over time, they looked forward to his visits. When he was off, they asked where he was and if he'd be back.

Driving a Meals on Wheels truck was a big switch from teaching chemistry. But talking to the families allowed Dick the job satisfaction he craved.

Giving back, making a difference, and helping others is a common theme for people living out their Retirement Reinvention today. Think about this: the world would be a much better place if every boomer decided to work five or ten hours a month to make society and our planet better. Can you even imagine the impact our generation might make by undertaking something so world-changing? *We'll get to lots of stories about people giving back in part 2.*

RETIREMENT MYTHS

Research by Merrill Lynch and Age Wave found that nearly half (47%) of today's retirees say they either have worked or plan to work during their retirement. But an even greater percentage (72%) of pre-retirees age fifty or older say they want to keep working after they retire. Indeed, this study highlighted how our long-held beliefs about retirement are changing:

Myth 1: Retirement means the end of work.
Reality: Over seven in ten pre-retirees say they want to work in retirement. In the near future, it will be increasingly unusual for retirees not to work. This includes volunteer and paid jobs.

Myth 2: Retirement is a time of decline.
Reality: A new generation of working retirees is pioneering a more engaged and active retirement.

Myth 3: People primarily work in retirement because they need the money.
Reality: This research reveals that some work primarily for the money; many others are motivated by important nonfinancial reasons.

Myth 4: New career ambitions are for young people.
Reality: Working retirees are three times more likely than pre-retirees to be entrepreneurs.

Over your lifetime, you've likely had

eleven or twelve job or career changes — the Retirement Reinvention stage represents just one more new career change.

> FACT: In the near future it will become increasingly unusual for retirees not to work.

Why is there this need to work in your final life phase?

1. Longer life expectancy — the average person lives into their eighties.
2. Elimination of pensions for most workers.
3. Fear of economic instability — boomers like the idea of still having some employment income.
4. Boomers seek greater purpose, stimulation, and fulfillment in retirement.
5. The need for new friends and social connection.

Baby boomers are pioneering a more engaged and active retirement. This will allow them to incorporate fun work and leisure into a lifestyle that is rewarding and feels happy and worth living.

An important insight is that as you enter your fifties, your perspective begins to shift. Many people focus more on how they can make a difference and what will their legacy be. They see social problems and seek out ways to improve situations. After they retire, they may choose to volunteer, building homes for Habitat for Humanity, for example, or teaching English to immigrants. Many people choose to use their talents to give back to society by providing a service to others. Other people enjoy a "fun hobby" job or even start a new business. There are countless ways that you can look at the world and find worthwhile ways to help. You have too many talents just to sit around playing bingo and shuffleboard. And you've got a lot of days, weeks, months, and years to fill. Yes, you can play tennis or golf, swim, walk the beach, travel, but you may also need something more to keep your brain active and your spirits high — something that is important and matters to you.

The old "golden years" model of retirement — with endless days of idleness and lazily just doing "stuff" — does not have to be for you. You might have hit your later fifties and sixties, but you still have exciting and enjoyable times in front of you. You have the health to be active and surely don't want to become a depressed coach potato.

This new, final career stage is something you are doing to meet *your own needs*. What is imperative is that it be one you chose because:

1. It's meaningful.
2. It gives you a sense of purpose.
3. It offers social interactions and a sense of community.
4. It's very interesting to you.
5. It's something you enjoy!

That's exactly how this book will help you shape your future. Instead of easing into a "leisure only" stage, I'm recommending you move to a new "fun job and leisure" stage. I'm naming this new and final stage of your career: *Retirement Reinvention.* Too often, we only consider the financial aspects of retirement. We don't plan for our lives beyond our jobs, and we become failed retirees, often suffering from depression, boredom, loneliness, and loss of purpose. Yet many of us have a mental list of things we always wanted but never had the time to do. Ask yourself whether that list is an accurate reflection of who you are today and what you want to do now. It's wise to actually sit down and write out the list you have in your head. Give it a hard look. Some things you will still want to do. Others will drop off your list as you realize that you are not the same person you were ten or fifteen years ago. You have changed, and your life goals need to be updated too.

The Retirement Reinvention stage offers you a new way to retire, with the opportunity to find work — paid or unpaid, full- or part-time — and to create meaning and enjoyment after your traditional career has ended. Many of us will have one, two, or three decades of good health after we retire. We need to create a plan for them, and for most of us that plan will include some form of work, but in a new, different arena. This book offers many retirees' stories, to inspire ideas you have yet to even consider for moving happily into retirement.

CHANGING RETIREMENT TRENDS FOR BABY BOOMERS

A fifty-seven-year-old, soft-spoken man, Jim, had spent his entire career as an aerospace engineer for the same Fortune 500 company. He specialized in testing composite materials to determine strength and bendability in a specialized wind tunnel — one of only three in the world — something that only a handful of engineers are capable of doing. Several years ago, I advised Jim, as his career coach, when he applied for (and got) a significant promotion to engineering test manager. Last year, his company began offering early retirement to older engineers and IT specialists. The package of incentives was designed to encourage voluntary participation. Although rumors that layoffs would follow if the older folks didn't leave ran rampant in the halls and by the coffee machines, Jim says, "I just assumed that my unique specialty provided me with job security, so I declined the offer of early retirement, kept working hard, and ignored what was happening around me."

Six months later, he was laid off — without any of the extra incentives. When HR first gave him the news, Jim says, "I was shocked. Then I got really angry that the company let me go after I'd been such a great employee. Finally, I got past that, but I quickly learned that no one wanted to hire a semi-bald, white-haired engineer whose specialized skills weren't even up-to-date or broad enough for contract work. Boy, it was so depressing."

Unfortunately, Jim's job had quit him, not the other way around. His engineering career was done, and slowly he accepted that he was retired, if not by choice. As I helped him find his way in this new stage, we talked about what his retirement could be. He had few outside interests but did enjoy learning and sharing his knowledge. While we narrowed down the possibilities for fulfilling but less stressful work, he kept returning to the idea of teaching. He decided to take a class on how to teach a college course and loved every minute. Jim now teaches at the local community college — retired but still contributing. He has found a new identity in being a professor. He isn't earning nearly as much money as before, but his level of satisfaction is just as high as it was.

Little did Jim know, but he was on the cutting edge of a change in retirement. Having your job quit you is a new trend: many boomers will find themselves in Jim's shoes. The company decides that its older workers need to go and that somehow they will find a way to do just that. Then, after losing their jobs and being unable to replace them, the new retirees need to reshape their lives into something other than being depressed and full of self-pity. In my career-counseling sessions, the epiphany usually comes when the retiree begins to see that the world holds many opportunities and chances to blend leisure with fulfilling work. And in a combination that fits one's needs. Finding a new passion and interest led Jim, for example, to a part-time job that engaged him intellectually and made him feel productive and happy again.

Retirement can happen for one of these reasons:

1. You choose to retire and do so on your own terms.
2. You are burned-out, tired of, dislike, or just done with your current career, so you quit.
3. Your career quits you because of outdated skills and/or your age.
4. You are "forced" to retire because the company wants you gone.

"We moved too much for me to keep a job as a military wife," says Marge, "so I stayed home and raised the children." When her husband left the military and they had a permanent residence, she got a job as paraeducator in an elementary school. She loved working with young children and had a big, compassionate heart for special-needs kids. Marge spent eleven years working as an aide to disabled kids.

But the school district had a mandatory retirement age of sixty-five. "I don't think

I'd have ever left my job if I hadn't been forced out," says Marge. "I realized later that I had made a serious mistake. I didn't have a purpose when I left my career. That really hurt me when I retired. Looking back, I wish I had a better plan. I suffered a lot of depression when I was not working in a classroom anymore. It took me a few years to begin to fill my life up with tasks that meant something. It sure was difficult to replace all I felt I lost when I left that job behind."

Most companies do not have a mandatory retirement age, but that doesn't mean they want their older workers to remain. In fact, Tom, a senior executive at HP, summed it up this way: "We are so top-heavy with boomers who are getting big paychecks but aren't contributing the way we need. If they don't leave, people can't move into their jobs and start that domino effect of promotions. Our company has let over eighty thousand people go, but we need to push out tens of thousands more so we can be innovative and bring in younger people with drive and fresh ideas."

Many of today's Fortune 500 companies feel the same way — they want older baby boomers to leave. I teach at a large company that has over one hundred thousand employees, and it has been seriously working toward pushing the older technical and engineering staff out. The company calls it "voluntary retirement," but as John found, it felt more like a big shove.

John had been employed at this company, as a planner, for most of his career. He was a top-paid employee and had had several promotions over the years. When the offer to take voluntary retirement came out, John's manager took him aside and said, "You should take this package and retire. The company is offering severance, and if you skip this offer, you could find yourself unemployed in six months with no extra money to go — they will just lay you off." John felt the pressure to go, and he appreciated that his boss cared enough to clue him in on how the future might go if he didn't accept the package and leave.

John had seen the company laying off older workers for two years under the guise of "reorganization." He says, "I did not want to leave, but I'm not stupid. I understood that the future at work was over, so I took the money and within six weeks I was officially 'retired.' "

How a Company Can Push You Out

Many people in senior management believe that baby boomers need to leave their jobs so other employees below them can move up. The conflict is that many boomers still need or want the paycheck, since they will likely live longer. After the last recession, many do need to save more before they are done with work. Organizations have found several tricky ways to get around union rules and seniority and discrimination policies, to push you out. These tactics include:

- Layoffs
- Job elimination (your job, at your level and salary, disappears)
- Your boss writing you up for a sudden performance drop
- Offering early retirement with incentives to leave (e.g., paid medical insurance)
- Instituting a mandatory retirement age
- Reducing job duties
- Stopping advanced-level work
- Cutting hours
- Assigning job duties you aren't equipped to perform

If the company wants you gone, it will find

a way. Some tactics are nice, such as offering severance pay and medical insurance, and others are just a way to fire you, often with nothing extra as you go out the door.

Don't kid yourself and think this won't happen to you. Kathleen was a terrific worker, with regular promotions and stellar performance reviews. In her early sixties, she planned to work for a few more years. Then the company changed her job. She lost most of her advanced work and was given menial and tedious technical activities to do. She got a new, young boss, and life got hard very fast. The boss constantly picked on her for being too slow. He gave her the worst assignments in the department. His performance review rated her "poor" and said she must improve in several areas or be fired. She got a mentor and a technical tutor, but even as she strived to make improvements the boss criticized her work. Within four months of the first "poor" performance review, he fired her, with no severance pay and only self-paid medical insurance. She was terribly depressed and felt betrayed by a company she had worked hard for over many years.

Almost every week the news reports a large company announcing a major layoff. The first people to go out the door will be

33

those the company views as expendable — most will be baby boomers.

You need to be on the lookout for these kinds of company tactics. If the writing is on the wall — see it! Do not be in denial. You need to be proactive to get the best exit option you can. Kathleen should have tried to go to her boss and offer to retire in exchange for severance pay and paid health-care insurance. She was in deep denial that the firing would ever happen. But happen it did.

> The gift of life is yours, but you are responsible for the quality of it.

THE ROAD AHEAD

Living longer means having plenty of time to do new, fun things. I talked with many retired boomers at the Creative Aging conference and quickly discovered how many retirees leave work with no plan and no clear to-do list.

In the new retirement world, Retirement Reinvention will be the final phase of a person's professional life. The Society for Human Resource Management has predicted that 72% of pre-retirees will have some form of work during the Retirement Reinvention phase of their life. The other

28% of boomers who retire will go straight to the end of the working phase and won't plan to have any more work in their lives. This latter group may change their minds after a year or so and seek out some form of volunteer or paid job.

This chart shows the stages of the old "golden years" path versus the new Retirement Reinvention path:

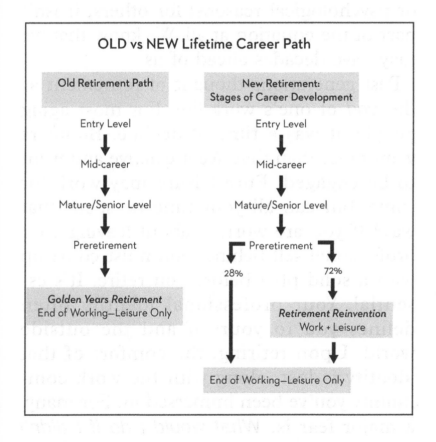

With long years ahead of us after we leave our careers, we don't want our parents'

retirement. The idea that we'll spend our postwork years traveling to warmer climes in the winter, spending our days playing golf or mahjong, and visiting our children and friends, is no longer enough. We want a meaningful, fun job to add into that mix, one that will give us a good reason to get up in the morning. For some, earning money is important, whether for financial or psychological reasons; for others, it isn't part of the equation at all. We know that we may have decades ahead of us.

Past generations thought of retirement as the *end* of one's work life. For most aging people, it was a time of decline. Boomers want more than that. We are active and want to be engaged. Pure leisure may work for some, but can all your time be spent that way? If you are worried about leaving your professional self behind, you must come up with a solid plan before you retire. It's essential. Your professional identity often defines you to yourself and the outside world. Upon retiring, the comfort of that identity is lost, along with the work community you've been immersed in. For many, a major fear is, *What would I do if I didn't work?* Other key concerns are:

- What about my identity? Who will I be?
- What about my desire to be productive and important in my own eyes?
- What about my emotional well-being?
- Who will I hang out with?
- What will I do with another twenty to thirty years still to live?

Your answers to these questions are the start of creating this new life, of reinventing your retirement as a final career stage. By considering a future in which you begin a *fun* job in something new and interesting, you can keep your mind active, your disposition pleasant, and meet new friends with similar interests.

How, you may be thinking, *do I define new, satisfying work that feels meaningful but may be part-time, flexible, and quite different from what I did before retiring?*

Working with my clients, I have developed a Retirement Reinvention program to help those in the preretirement stage or those who have become stuck after leaving their job to create a new direction. This program is the basis of this book and the key to helping you plan how you want to spend your postcareer years. It also shows you how to make it happen.

In the upcoming chapters, you'll experience my Retirement Reinvention program. It begins by helping you navigate the process of how to leave your old career behind. Without this essential step, you may find yourself stuck, not knowing who you can become after decades of being defined by your work. I will guide you through a review of your current skills, and we'll explore your values, hobbies, and interests. This step is the basis for defining new, satisfying work — work that feels meaningful but is different from your current (or previous) work. You'll explore not only what you want to do, focusing on a fun new situation, but also *how* you want to do it: start a new business, volunteer, consult, work full- or part-time? You'll learn how to manage your leisure and work schedules, assessing how much time you want to devote to each. And you'll consider issues such as how much money you need to earn, where you are going to live (staying put, moving to a new community, living in two different places over the course of each year?). The answers to these questions will define what kind of work you want to incorporate as you design your own Retirement Reinvention. Throughout this book, I'll share stories that show the different options real people have used to achieve happiness and fulfillment during their Retirement Reinventions. These stories will help percolate new ideas and inspire a wide variety of ways you can create the ideal life for yourself.

MY JOB HAS BEEN MY LIFE — SO NOW WHAT?

Some people *are* their job. Many of us get a sense of worth, recognition, respect, and power from our work and the positions we hold. This has been true for men for years — their whole identity can be based in their job title and prestige from the positions they hold. Women have experienced this too, especially as they have risen to positions of control and power. As corporate America downsizes, however, former VPs, managers, executives, and CEOs feel the loss profoundly. These people suddenly find themselves heads of nothing. They lose their identities, and sometimes themselves.

A highflier in the three large pharmaceutical companies she'd worked for, Colleen had been a regional sales manager and then moved up to the executive director spot when her husband, Bob, got cancer at age fifty-eight. This was a fun-loving, teddy bear of a man who loved life and enjoyed experiences, travel, socializing, and parties. Over the next three years, Colleen watched her beloved husband fade away. At sixty-one, Bob's life was over. In her early fifties, Colleen's whole view of life changed. "I was alone, with no children, and losing my husband had a profound effect on me," she says.

First, she recognized that she no longer needed to earn as much income as possible. If her money was well invested, she could retire and have a great life. "I realized life was not about the next project and sales numbers. It should be about being with family, living life, and making memories," explains Colleen.

At fifty-six she left work. Now, three years later, she is busy with her volunteer commitments. She met a wonderful man and recently married him. To celebrate turning sixty, they went on an African safari.

"The safari had been a far-off dream," says this vibrant woman. "It had been on my bucket list. So we decided to go. It was unbelievable. I'll admit it was very expensive, but I want to experience things now. I'm really healthy and fit, so I plan to do the activities and see the sights I never had time for when I worked, and I want to do them all now, while I can."

Giving back is also important to Colleen.

She averages about fifteen hours a week working at two different charities. They make her feel like she is doing something meaningful.

"In my work role, I was never removed from the office before. It was work, work, work. I'd go on a short vacation and always did e-mails and returned business calls. Now," Colleen declares, "I am so free! It's a luxurious experience. But I have learned that time is so precious and things can change on a dime. I'm making the most of my retired days."

Career and personal identity are very closely linked for people who, like Colleen, work a great deal. Doctors, lawyers, CPAs, architects, dentists, executives, engineers, and professionals — many of these people have devoted their lives to their professions. They have loved doing their work. Some have been workaholics, spending sixty or more hours a week at a demanding job. Many do not know how to live outside their professional worlds. Many are scared to retire. Although they may be tired or burned-out, they find the fear of the emptiness ahead of them if they leave their current job too overwhelming to face.

Am I describing you? If so, your future requires some definite planning and new ideas. The Retirement Reinvention process you are about to go through will help you uncover some new interests and a new way to live and enjoy your life after you leave your current career behind. No, it won't be the same. Endings happen — sometimes, unfortunately, before you want them. Keep in mind that almost all of us *will retire.* You will lose the job (as well as the stress, hassles, politics, and commute). The perks will disappear. Work acquaintances will go on networking but no longer include you. Hanging on won't make it easier. To become a successful retiree, you need a new game plan, a solid direction that makes you feel excited about living this new stage of life. Retirement Reinvention is essential for your future well-being.

GETTING STARTED

First you need to reflect and do a bit of soul-searching to uncover what would make your future happy. Begin by answering these questions. Let's assume you are still working as you approach these key questions.

What would I miss most from my current career?

_____

_____

How do I define my professional identity?

_____

_____

_____

_____

What are my thoughts about losing my position of power and success once I retire?

_____

_____

_____

_____

What feelings must I get from retirement to make it feel worthwhile?

_____

_____

_____

_____

Is there a cause or particular interest I might like to pursue once I retire?

_____

_____

_____

_____

What is my top *reason for not retiring today?*

_____

_____

_____

_____

The first two big *things I want to do when I retire are:*

1._____

2._____

Retirement Reinvention requires you to examine what you will leave behind and miss. If it is social connection and community, then you must replace them with a new group of people who have the same interests you do. If you have enjoyed a hobby or have a consuming interest, you can find a way to become immersed in it. The chapters ahead will help you successfully retire into a happy, desirable life — one you want to live.

LIFE INTRUSIONS

The road to Retirement Reinvention varies. Brenda was a CPA and had been a CFO, when she got sick and was shoved into retirement. Then she got divorced, found new love, and remarried. She also got caught up in caring for her aging parents. At sixty-one, this former career-counseling client called me because, after five years of dealing with these life interruptions, she wanted to work again. During our session, it became evident that her career in finance was likely over. Finance is an unforgiving field that does not tolerate long gaps of unemployment. Brenda didn't seem to have the desire to undergo the intense reeducation it would take to get her back up to speed.

So we talked about a meaningful retirement option. She admitted that she had been considering another option. When I asked what she was thinking about, she said, "I love business etiquette and protocol. I've researched this career option and found a school that offers the top training in the United States. It is expensive, at nearly seven thousand dollars, plus travel and hotel expenses, for the five-day program." This was an intriguing idea, but she still had no plan. She lived in Idaho. Could she pull this work off there? Who would hire her? I had her look into the program more thoroughly and get some references from recent grads. Apparently, the original owner and program director had died and the new people running the program weren't doing that good a job. I encouraged her to network and conduct some research. From other people doing this work, found on LinkedIn, Brenda learned a lot about the pros and cons of this job, the skills she needed to excel, the best training options, who might hire her or buy her services, which services to offer, how to price them, who offered the best training with the top connections, and how to successfully launch her business.

We determined this new role would be a part-time job and probably not a consistent moneymaker. But Brenda said that was okay. No longer scared that this was a fanciful idea, she worked with me to make a written plan that included getting educated, developing a website, and networking heavily with people in the industry and her old contacts to launch her Retirement Reinvention. Indeed, self-discovery, good research and investigation, plus enacting a reasonable plan, made all the difference and allowed her to succeed.

Today Brenda uses technology to advance her protocol business. "Using a free online video and audio recording service allows me to do my job from anywhere. I can find clients worldwide to offer my services to. Technology has allowed me to do consulting and not have to travel much — it's worked out very nicely," she says.

DON'T BE A FAILED RETIREE

Did you know you can fail at retirement? Well, you certainly can.

Dennis was a doctor who had become tired of his medical practice. Health care was changing so much and the reduced income, work stress, and pressure had gotten to be too much. He felt drained and decided to sell his practice, thinking he and his wife could retire now that his kids had finished college. The couple took a cruise around the world, which she had always wanted to do. They enjoyed it. After returning, his wife went to lunch with friends and to yoga classes every day, leaving Dennis to fend for himself. He had spent so much time working as a physician, he had few outside interests besides reading novels. Golf and tennis were out, since he suffered from a bad knee. Within six months, he was too bored and depressed to remain at home anymore. He started looking into temporary medical positions, yet these full-time jobs put him back in the stressful environment he had left behind. Frustrated and disillusioned, he just could not see any other options. Medicine had been his life — his

47

entire world. He spent his retirement floundering, depressed and unsatisfied. Dennis had, in fact, failed as a retiree. This could be you. Without an action plan for your retirement, you might also turn into an unhappy coach potato.

If you have been a workaholic, or a business owner, you stand a pretty strong chance of failing in retirement. Work has been the center of your universe. Certainly, you have gained a lot from your labors — success, prestige, meaning, and income. It can definitely be a struggle to find new joy and meaning when you leave your professional self behind. Unless you want to find yourself job hunting a year after you retire, you need a solid plan. This is what you will be working on as you go through the chapters ahead. Ideally, you should develop some outside interests before you leave work, but you can always explore new things once you are retired. New goals and lifestyle changes will enable you to make the transition successfully. For some people, getting retirement coaching is an excellent idea.

A very successful businesswoman, Sunny was an attractive, powerful lady who had acquired a lot of prestige. She sold her company at the age of forty-two. She and her husband were left with what you and I would call extreme wealth and never needed to worry about money again. She did have to fret about this new retirement though. The couple traveled a lot, but Sunny found her days too isolating when she was home for a long spell. We met, and I suggested she find a hobby or charity at which to volunteer. She supported many charities financially, but when it came to thinking about working at one, she wondered what to do. I got her talking about her personal interests. "I love large wild animals — cats in particular: tigers, leopards, jaguars, and lions. I once did a certification course at a facility that trains large animals for the movies. During the course of that training, I got to work closely with those exquisite cats, and I was fascinated," Sunny proclaimed.

I suggested she look into working at a zoo in the large cat areas. She found something better than that: an outdoor sanctuary near her winter home, which took in animals, large and small, that had been injured in the wild. The vets treated them, but these animals would not be able to return to the wild. This animal sanctuary used volunteers. Sunny assumed it would be easy to get a spot working directly with the large cats. Her first revelation was that volunteering was going to be a lot harder than she'd imagined. Like many places, the facility preferred year-round volunteers. A snowbird, Sunny spent only five months in the area.

"It took some serious persuasion with the volunteer director to give me a chance at working at the sanctuary," she says. "My first winter, I took the training necessary to work there. I got nowhere near my beloved animals. The next season, I got some tasks that involved helping clean out cages and preparing the food. All part of the work, but still not exactly what I was looking for," she explains.

The sanctuary uses volunteers to run an educational tour program. Sunny offered to do that. She learned each of the animals' names and how they came to be at the sanctuary. She excelled at leading tours for the groups who came to learn about the animals. Part of the tour includes giving treats to the animals so they will come up to the fence and guests can get a closer look at the various cats, bears, and other animals who call the sanctuary home. It was a win for both Sunny and the facility. She is a very popular guide, and there are lots of positive reviews on TripAdvisor and Yelp from enthusiastic guests who've taken her tours.

"I work part-time around my beloved

jaguars, mountain lions, bears, and more, so I couldn't be happier," Sunny shares.

Even if you have all of the money in the world, you will still have to work to create your best Retirement Reinvention.

BETTER DAYS ARE AHEAD

Begin today. Continue to read this book to develop a plan for your retirement. Then, if you do get shoved out the door, you will have a better place to land and make the next stage of life more palatable. You'll see opportunities you hadn't thought of. You'll hear interesting stories of what others are doing. You'll get practical tools to assist you in making better decisions.

Your new future will include doing meaningful, fun work — likely part-time. You can still earn money if that is your goal. Or you may elect to work in a volunteer capacity. You have some truly wonderful options to choose from. One career will end — yes, everything ends — but your future will be what you choose to make it. Working together, we will set a new course for happy days and enjoyment ahead.

So many retirees are reshaping their lives. As you read on, keep your mind open! Try not to be negative about every idea suggested, but instead look and see if it might be a possibility for you. Too many times people think about why they *can't* do things instead of figuring out how they *can.* Sunny's dream was not an easy one to obtain. It took time to find the animal sanctuary and over two years to work in there before she got near the large cats. Dick took the Meals on Wheels job to be useful. Only after he had done it for a while did he discover the joy of chatting about his former students with the elderly people he delivered meals to. Brenda had a dream, but it took guts, good planning, and new training to turn her fantasy into a whole new business.

Your attitude will impact your ability to have a meaningful retirement. Explore! Be open to the new ideas you'll read about in this book. Look ahead and see yourself living a meaningful and happy life. You will define what that will look like as we go through this book. It must be something personally satisfying and fulfilling. That will be our top goal in developing your meaningful and enjoyable retirement plan.

Retirement Reinvention should be viewed as another phase — a happy stage — of your life and career. See it as the days when you will meet new people, many quite interesting. You'll share common interests with these new friends. You will be doing different, important work that you want to do and that makes you happy. The engineer loves teaching — something he would never have done if he hadn't retired. For him, and for you, this new stage is not an end but a continuation of the last stage of your career. It can — and should — be a joyous time of your life. Pay close attention to what your heart says. Visualize some new dreams. Allow us to work together — you partnering with me — to build you a new life plan that makes the days ahead happy ones.

Let's get started!

CHAPTER 2
WHAT DO YOU WANT TO DO NOW?

If it is to be, it is up to me.

"I don't want to die without having really *lived* all the stages of my life," says Catherine, a former CEO of a premier boutique consulting firm, who sold her company at age fifty-nine. "I loved my job, and I want to love my retirement too. I looked *fear* in the face — yes, I was scared to sell my business and retire — but I sold it anyway. It was a big risk, but I have also found that when I do take risks, that is when I have the most personal growth."

Sitting on the sidelines or becoming a TV-watching homebody was not on Catherine's agenda. She wanted to fulfill a few dreams she had not been able to get to when working. For starters, she began to learn Spanish. Being a global citizen and someone who has traveled extensively, she felt diminished only knowing one language. It was really hard to learn a new language at her age. But she was doing it anyway.

Catherine also had a childhood dream she had never fulfilled. She had always wanted to sing. "As a child I was the oldest of seven children," she explains. "And when I told my mom that I wanted to stay after school and join the chorus, the answer was a very loud and repeated no. There were kids to babysit and diapers to change, and so I grew up feeling bitter that I could not participate in any singing groups."

Fast-forward to last year, when an old childhood friend told her, via Facebook, about a choral group in the Seattle-area community where Catherine lives. She went, tried out, and was accepted as a singer. That group just sang at Carnegie Hall in New York City. "Carnegie Hall was amazing!" Catherine told me, smiling from ear to ear. "We had a standing ovation from an almost full house of twenty-five hundred people. It was an aha! experience and just shows that my best days are not behind me."

Whereas Catherine took the retirement bull by the horns and found an immediate way to make herself feel happy and fulfilled, most people do not start off their retirement that way. One man posted the following on a career website:

I just took early retirement from my company at age fifty-seven. I loved my work, but because the twenty- and thirtysomethings were taking over, I felt I had no choice but to leave. My last year there was horrible. So, I gave up and retired. Now I feel so angry and cheated! I'm a workaholic! I loved working! Who decided that when you hit a certain age you are no longer needed? My brain still works fine! I'm looking for a new job, but I see the age discrimination thing everywhere I go. I've been "retired" for exactly one month and I'm climbing the walls! I'm really getting tired of housework, but that's all I have to do. I have no hobbies. My job was my life. I'm becoming more and more depressed every day. I feel so useless. I don't think my life should be considered over at age fifty-seven, but it seems to be. I tell people I'm retired and their eyes glass over like I'm completely irrelevant now. Do I have to accept that my life is over? My self-esteem is so far down, I don't know if I can ever feel good about myself again. There are days that I wish I could just go to sleep and never wake up. The whole world would probably be better off . . . I seem to be just "taking up space" here.

Wow — this man needs career counseling and a good retirement plan! Yet if you read through his complaints, you can hear the thoughts many other people think too. This explains why many end up retired and miserable — "failed retirees."

Trainer and coach Dori Gillam of Positive Endings (www.dorigillam.com) specializes in working with people over sixty. She has a mile-deep understanding of baby boomers facing retirement. She teaches people that they need to change the way they envision retirement.

Usually, she says, "It's really just aging, not retiring." The one big question she asks boomers to consider is, *Who are you going to be as you age?* Dori points out, "People need to do a bit more in retirement than they thought they might, to shake it up a bit and try something new. They need to think hard about *what will I do when I no longer work to live?* The typical response is often, 'Are you kidding? I'm going to play tennis,' or golf or lie on the beach. That plan, then, is to do nothing. The trouble with doing nothing is that you never know when you're done! There is so much more to consider. How will you contribute? What will you learn? Whom will you teach? You'll have plenty of time to lie on the beach, but you also need to think about how you will nourish your soul."

Kate Westin, organizational consultant with CWA Connect, works with executives and professionals on various behavioral issues including dealing with boomers close to retiring. "There is a lot of concern about facing the biggest change of your life. For many individuals," she explains, "there is the concern of feeling 'irrelevant' once you retire — that society won't see you as important as you were before."

In my own work, I have seen that my clients' need for relevance can dramatically intensify once they lose their work identity, workplace colleagues, and access to professional development. Nobody wants to become obsolete or to be perceived as disconnected or unproductive, especially baby boomers, who may feel irrelevance runs contrary to everything they stand for and have sought to achieve. Most people who feel irrelevant assume that society made them that way, but that's not the case. You make yourself irrelevant by your own negative thoughts. This book is designed to positively motivate you by offering hundreds of new ideas you can implement. But the feeling that you have value must come from inside you. Taking action to create a new life — a fun and worthwhile life — will keep you from feeling irrelevant. You'll have too many important things to do.

DON'T FIXATE

Many people obsess about the financial aspects of retirement: How will we pay the bills? Do we have enough in our pension or 401(k)? What happens if we become ill? What happens if our Social Security runs out? It's not that these questions aren't important — in fact, they are, and we'll explore them in chapter 4. Many retirement books and articles dwell on the money part of retirement. This book is different. Sadly, few boomers spend much time thinking about *what they will do* to fill the days that stretch empty and unstructured ahead of them. It quickly became clear to me that I needed to offer career coaching focused on how to fill your days meaningfully for years to come. That is a key question, and answering it requires some serious self-analysis. *If I retire, what will I do?* That is the elephant in the room. We fear not knowing. We fear being irrelevant and alone. In essence, we are scared of a major life change. This is why it's important, as you look ahead, to have a good, well-structured plan you feel excited to live out.

Bill, a recent career counseling client and owner of a boutique accounting firm, told me, "I spent my work life solely focused on my job. My wife says I was a workaholic. Really? I took great pride in the work I did as a CPA. Sure, I worked a lot of hours, but you do when you own the business and it's your name on the door. I really feel desperate about leaving my work identity behind, which is why the whole retirement thing is driving me nuts. *What am I going to do? How will I matter? Who will I be?* I don't have a clue as to how I can rechannel myself and make my retirement as good as my work life has been. I think most successful people may really suck at this 'business life to retirement' transition. My brother retired last year, after being a lawyer his whole life, and he's miserable. Feels like he is a has-been and can't find a new road for this life stage. I do not want that to be me."

Too often we try to replicate our careers by hanging out a shingle as a consultant or a speaker. It often doesn't work out and leads to a lot of frustration and even depression. Type As and high achievers do need to rechannel themselves and to learn how to let go of the anxiety and drive that fueled their work lives. That doesn't mean life is over. On the contrary, retirement is a time to set new goals that ensure you avoid boredom yet don't recreate the stress of your former career.

Whether you were married to your career, just got tired, left because the company wanted you gone, or the job was simply a way of bringing home a paycheck, you still need a reason to get up in the morning once you begin your Retirement Reinvention.

What's that elephant in the room?

Let's address one of the big "elephant in the room" challenges: fear of becoming irrelevant or even invisible. Start by asking yourself these key questions:

- Who will I *be* after I retire?
- What will I do?
- What's the one thing I haven't done yet because I'm afraid?

In retirement, your identity may need to be redefined. You need new dreams, new goals, and fun, exciting things to look forward to. Unconscious limiting beliefs may prevent you from doing things you could really enjoy. What prevents you from going after your dreams? You may not have given yourself permission to pursue what you really want. Some folks believe they don't have the right to be fully alive and happy. That isn't true! You need to focus on planning a better future for yourself *now*. One that allows you to be fully alive and happy.

Developing a happier retirement starts with some serious soul-searching. You need to begin to think about the questions above and also to try to answer the questions below. You may want to get a journal or dedicated notepad. First contemplate your answers and then write them down. Consider these questions:

- What do you *really* want to do?
- What is meaningful to you now?
- What makes you happy?
- What have you done recently that was really fun?
- How important is making a difference to you?
- Do you care about leaving a legacy behind?
- How do you deal with ambiguity?
- What things haven't you tried but secretly would like to?
- How do you create an intentional life?

These are some heady questions to think about. But now is the time to *face your fears* so a new you can emerge.

ADAPTABILITY IS KEY

Consider how you manage change. Easily? With great difficulty? Somewhere in between? Leaving work for retirement is a major, major change. Many people overidentify with their job and have to remind themselves that after they retire they *still have value, still have a lot to offer,* and that *there is so much yet to experience and do.* You may need to repeat this as a new mantra, because deep down inside many people are afraid of being irrelevant. Fear keeps them working, when, instead, they could be planning something new, different, and fun for themselves.

Make a conscious choice to think about your own life ahead. Forget about limits for a moment. What haven't you done yet? What fun things do you want to do? How do you create a life you *want* to live?

What are two things in life you want to do and will definitely regret not doing?

1._____

2._____

Now you have two activities, experiences, or missions that need to be completed. Now go back and write in *when* you want to have completed these things. Make it sooner rather than later.

Do you have a bucket list? If not, create one here. If you do, look it over and revise it so it is current and reflects the things you still want to accomplish or experience in your lifetime. Fill this bucket list with your dreams, goals, and ambitions. Dream big!

BUCKET LIST

"How do you plan on spending your retirement?" These pursuits appeared in the following percentage of answers to this question:

Travel: 55%
Spend more time with family: 52%
Volunteer work: 34%
Take up a hobby: 34%
Work (full- and part-time): 34%
Spend time with friends: 30%
Continue education: 7%
Start a business: 5%

Source: *USA Today*

Here are the ten things I definitely want to do before I die:

1. _____

2. _____

3. _____

4. _____

5. _____

6. _____

7. _____

8. _____

9. _____

10. _____

As you look ahead, you need to create a new life that has a purpose — something that makes getting up in the morning worthwhile. You need to consider what you are going to do with your time. As you cruise into this final career stage, *having some meaningful work* — truly feeling satisfied by what you do — is key to retirement success. You'll have more joy and a better life if you have meaningful work as a part of your retired life. Keep in mind that this doesn't mean the same old job you are leaving behind.

As part of their Retirement Reinvention, many people take on new jobs in a whole different arena. Something fun! They mostly select stress-free jobs that bring them into contact with a lot of people, because in retirement it often becomes necessary to make new friends and seek out new social connections.

You might, for example, take a hobby you love and turn that into a new career. The trends point to many boomers working in part-time jobs — some paid, others volunteer. But many boomers see the need to have an important and worthwhile purpose in their lives, and this comes from some form of work.

The goal for your Retirement Reinvention is this: seek out work that's *different* from your old career. Do something new, in a new field. Find something that's a source of fun, with social interaction and satisfaction. Consider something enriching and enjoyable that you can do with like-minded people.

A TINY BIT OF COUPLES THERAPY

In retirement, couples face unique problems they likely have not encountered before.

Have you and your spouse discussed how each of you will spend your days once you are retired?

In my professional experience, this is a subject people don't talk or think about enough. As a couple, you very likely have not had 24-7 time together for decades. Once you are both retired, you will. What does that new life look like? Each spouse really needs to think about this.

One thing that seems to cause serious problems is selling one's home too fast. If you sell and move away, you don't just get rid of the house but also leave behind your friends, network, doctors, clubs, and all the connections you've built over the years. All this can be hard to replace in a new region.

Moving: Beware!

Betsy shares her frustration with moving: "*Moving is a big deal,* a much bigger deal socially than I had considered. I wish I could move back. I hate my new neighborhood and how I know no one." Betsy sold and downsized, moving from one side of the city to another — about fifteen miles away. "I didn't think it would be a problem, but once I moved I realized it was like starting all over again. It was so awful. No neighbors next door to chat with. No close friends just a minute or two away. Not knowing the church. And of course I never considered how much the traffic would interfere with seeing old friends." Keep in mind that moving anywhere is a *big* change.

TIME TO PLAN

Let's begin the career-counseling process of planning out your retirement by taking my proprietary retiring values assessment, interest inventory, and hobbies prioritization test. This will help you envision your own future more clearly.

Let's investigate what matters to you now, at this stage of your life. What are you interested in? What kinds of people do you wish to surround yourself with? What kinds of fun jobs or small businesses can you move into and remain happy and vibrant in, living life to its fullest when you are retired?

How do you envision spending your retirement days? Check any that apply.

❒ Leisure
❒ Volunteer work (unpaid)

- ❐ Service work — paid or unpaid (circle one)
- ❐ Paid job
- ❐ Start a business

VALUES ASSESSMENT

Our values change over time. Let's determine exactly what matters the most to you at this age. Review the values listed below and circle the five most important for your Retirement Reinvention.

Acquiring new knowledge	Adventure
Advocacy	Being around interesting people
Being your own boss	Challenging work
Developing a legacy	Earning a salary
Flexibility	Freedom from pressure and stress
Friendships	Helping others
Interacting with the public	Learning a new skill

Leisure time	Making a difference
More time with family	Outdoor work
Part-timework	Peacefulness
Physical work	Power and influence
Producing something new	Recognition
Security	Status and prestige
Supervising others	Teaching others
Travel opportunities	Using my mind
Using my creativity	Working from home
Working from anywhere	Working with others

Values are motivators. Now list the five values you circled, in order of importance:

1. _____

2. _____

3. _____

4. _____

5. _____

Next, examine how you want to balance your time using this leisure–work time assessment. The results will provide the building blocks for our Retirement Reinvention plan.

One week has 168 hours. Decide how you plan to spend them.

My Retired Week (168 Hours)
Let's begin by subtracting the basics:

- Sleep (58 hours, or approximately 8.25 hours a night) = 110 hours left
- Eating (approximately 10 hours, according to the Department of Agriculture) = 100 hours left

Now, what are you going to do with your 100 hours each week? We all have the same amount of time. Be realistic and decisive about how you will use yours.

Divide the 100 hours of the week among the activities below (and note any other activities too).

- Work/volunteer time:_____
- Leisure time:_____
- TV watching:_____
- Newspaper/magazine/book reading: _____
- On computer/iPad/cell phone: _____
- Doing social media:_____
- Exercise:_____
- Dressing and bathing:_____
- Cooking:_____
- Obligations/chores/housework: _____
- Anything else:_____

DEFINE YOUR INTERESTS

*Do what you love simply because
it will make you happy.*

What turns you on? What makes you come alive and feel excited? It's *passion* we are looking for here. Blending your talents and interests is the secret formula for long-term retirement happiness.

Your objective is to define what you find interesting. Examine both personal and professional interests; let your mind roam, and record everything that comes into it: food, music, travel, online auctions —

anything you enjoy learning about, discussing, or doing.

How do people find fun jobs that they would love to do? They start by selecting an area in which they are interested. Let's take a look at your past and present hobbies. These can be very rewarding and lead to your postretirement career. Your passion can be a starting point. Here are a few examples.

When Kristen tired of the daily drain from her hospital social-work duties and was contemplating retirement, we uncovered her true passion: her artistic talents. She began to take some drawing and graphic design classes. She loved to create new things, especially illustrations and digital art. Today she works part-time at a nonprofit and creates artwork, graphics, and designs for its marketing materials and website. She earns a salary, not as high as before, but she loves the work. It equals out for her: happiness in exchange for a job she'd grown to hate.

A fitness buff who retired from the navy as an officer, Dave had no intention of returning to work. It came about though, when one day at the gym someone asked him for training help. He coached the man, who was impressed and offered to pay Dave to train him. "I had always worked out and studied the magazines and different routines," notes Dave, who ended up deciding to get certified as a fitness trainer. "I now have several clients. This job pays good money, but it's so much fun helping people improve their health and fitness, I'd do it for free."

Your Retirement Reinvention career may be born from pursuing hobbies or dreams. As we see from Dave and Kristen, they may even pay a salary. You may feel more comfortable doing something that brings in a paycheck. But also remember that when you work at something you love, it can enrich your whole life, making you and everyone around you happier.

Hang in here a bit longer if you have no hobbies or can't think of any to pursue. We've got a long list of ideas coming up.

WHY IS FINDING MEANINGFUL WORK IMPORTANT?

Meaningful activity will play a huge role in your retired life. If you feel bored, depressed, or unsatisfied with what you do for large parts of the day, it can take a serious toll on your physical and mental health.

Give some thought to things you enjoyed doing as a child and in your teen years. Often our truest passions emerge in childhood, only to be squelched by real-life pressures. Think about what you loved long before you had to worry about your career. Writing? Science experiments? Taking care of people? Getting back in touch with those instincts may be a helpful and important step in finding your retirement passion. In career counseling, when people want to change careers we often ask them: *If money were no object, what would you want to do?* That's the kind of fun and passion you should try to pursue in retirement.

If you are stuck, look through a college catalogue, especially at the continuing education classes. Which courses naturally interest you? Acting? Painting? Reading tarot cards? Car mechanics? Fine art? History? What courses do you think you could teach? Which subjects scare you to death, and which ones do you find boring? Revisiting these possibilities will help point you in the direction of subjects and topics you would love to know more about.

Once you have a solid idea of what you love doing, get online. Check out Facebook, Pinterest, or Twitter to uncover and connect with people who share your areas of interest. Read blogs, join forums, and find out what it's really like to do what attracts your interest. This time spent exploring should be both fun and useful. You'll get ideas about different jobs, groups, and potential employers as you pursue your interests.

"I had a pretty fun job because I really loved sports," says Greg, who was a writer for NBC Sports when he took an early retirement. His wife traveled, so he had lots of time to spend with his two very active teenage boys. Within a few years, however, he had too much time on his hands. "I needed to do something worthwhile," Greg says. "I decided to pursue another interest: politics. I had always followed the news and had strong views on key issues. I spent the next thirteen months working on a national campaign for a woman running for office. I loved the competitive strategy, the campaigning, and most of all I was aligned with the causes and values. I saw eye to eye on the issues with this candidate. So when the race was over, I'd had such a good experience I began to look for the next candidate I could volunteer to work for."

You are multifaceted too. Consider your interests and begin to explore a few. Need some ideas? Keep reading.

HOBBIES: MAKE $$$, TRY NEW THINGS

Chapple was a librarian who worked across from a large lake and took a ferry to work every day — a long but relaxing commute. At age sixty-one, she decided to retire.

"A couple years earlier, at work, I'd heard a very interesting presentation that caught my interest. It was by Anna Cummins, an Olympic rower who had won a gold medal in the 2008 Summer Olympics and a silver medal in the 2004 Summer Olympics. After listening to her presentation and getting to talk to her, I found a fascination with rowing that I never even knew I had before. I thought, *I should try to take some classes to learn to row.* But unfortunately my schedule just always conflicted, so that new hobby got tabled."

A few months into her retirement, she took a rowing class at the age of sixty-two. She was fascinated because many of the women in the class were in their sixties and seventies, and a few were even in their eighties. She said to herself, *I want that eighty-year-old out there rowing to be me.* She told me, "When I was working, my idea of an outside sport was to read a book under a tree. I have no athletic ability, and I had never done athletic activities because there really weren't any when I was growing up. So I took this rowing class and figured out that you either love it or it's not for you. And it's definitely for me. The group is a really wonderful bunch of old farts who really enjoy what they're doing. Luckily, it's a welcoming group, but you've got to pull your own weight. No one ever made fun of me because I didn't know what to do or I wasn't very good. Compared to many of them, I'm still not very good, but I love it because it gets me up every day and out on the water.

"Once you commit," Chapple explains, "you *have to show up.* You can't just say *I don't feel like doing it today.* For me, it's not about the exercise. I truly love rowing! It gives me a kind of Zen experience, focusing on each stroke, trying to make it perfect. And the next one perfect. So it's a unique experience, where you need to be focused on what you're doing and then the rest of the world seems to dissolve away."

Maybe something on the hobbies list below will catch your eye. If so, investigate it. Talk to people who do it. Try it out. Try a few out. And quit quickly if you find it's not for you. Then try something else. Retirement can have many new, fun activities in it. Enjoy the process of trying to find a few you'll love doing.

This is a partial list of hobbies you might want to pursue in your retirement. Check off any that seem like they might be of real interest.

- ☐ Animal care
- ☐ Attending concerts
- ☐ Auto racing
- ☐ Being in a car club (e.g., Corvettes)
- ☐ Billiards
- ☐ Blogging
- ☐ Book club
- ☐ Bridge
- ☐ Camping
- ☐ Chess
- ☐ Cigars
- ☐ Coloring (adult coloring books)
- ☐ Cooking
- ☐ Crocheting
- ☐ Dancing
- ☐ Dating online
- ☐ DIY home-improvement projects
- ☐ Entertaining
- ☐ Exercising
- ☐ Fantasy sports
- ☐ Fashion design

- ☐ Art
- ☐ Attending sporting events
- ☐ Being at the beach
- ☐ Bicycling

- ☐ Bird watching
- ☐ Boating
- ☐ Bowling
- ☐ Cake decorating
- ☐ Car restoration
- ☐ Church activities
- ☐ Collectibles
- ☐ Computer

- ☐ Crafts
- ☐ Cultural events
- ☐ Dating
- ☐ Dining out
- ☐ Electronic robots building

- ☐ Event planning
- ☐ Family time
- ☐ Fashion
- ☐ Fishing

- ❏ Football
- ❏ Gambling at a casino
- ❏ Gardening
- ❏ Genealogy
- ❏ Going on cruises
- ❏ Going to the gym
- ❏ Golf
- ❏ Grilling
- ❏ Gun shooting
- ❏ Hiking
- ❏ Home brewing beer
- ❏ Horseback riding
- ❏ Horses
- ❏ Housework
- ❏ Hunting
- ❏ Interior decorating
- ❏ Investing
- ❏ Jewelry design
- ❏ Knitting
- ❏ Learning something
- ❏ Learning to speak a foreign language
- ❏ Listening to music
- ❏ Making cookies
- ❏ Making pies
- ❏ Massage
- ❏ Meditation
- ❏ Motorcycling
- ❏ Movies
- ❏ New technology
- ❏ Painting (walls)
- ❏ Painting (pictures)
- ❏ Pets
- ❏ Philanthropy
- ❏ Planning parties
- ❏ Playing a musical instrument
- ❏ Playing cards
- ❏ Poker
- ❏ Politics
- ❏ Pottery
- ❏ Quilting
- ❏ Reading
- ❏ Relaxing
- ❏ Religion
- ❏ Rocketry (model rockets/airplanes)
- ❏ Running
- ❏ Sailing
- ❏ Scrapbooking
- ❏ Shopping
- ❏ Skiing
- ❏ Socializing

- ☐ Swimming
- ☐ Team sports
- ☐ Theater
- ☐ Video games
- ☐ Volunteering
- ☐ Walking
- ☐ Watching TV
- ☐ Wine tasting
- ☐ Working on cars
- ☐ Yoga
- ☐ Other_____

- ☐ Tai chi
- ☐ Tennis
- ☐ Travel
- ☐ Visiting national parks
- ☐ Walking on the beach
- ☐ Watching sports
- ☐ Wine and painting
- ☐ Woodworking
- ☐ Writing
- ☐ Zumba

Others ideas to consider:

- **Gardening:** master gardener, volunteer at city parks, florist, work at a plant nursery.
- **Pets:** dog trainer, pet walker, pet sitter, pet photographer, board animals while people are on vacation, grooming.
- **Writing:** novelist, blogger, ghostwriter, copywriter, freelance article writer, content developer, write social media for a business, author, speaker, editor, proofreader, teach writing.
- **Cooking:** teach cooking classes, create custom cakes, cater, be a rent-out chef for dinner parties, bake/sell pies,

sell cookies, create a cookbook, develop a recipe blog.

- **Shopping:** mystery shopper, retail job, personal shopper, bargain shopping, reselling.
- **Movies:** actor, become an extra in films or TV shows, work in production as part of a film crew.
- **Photography:** sell photos on online websites, charge for family or baby pictures, cover birthday parties, take youth sports pictures.
- **Sports:** coach, referee, sell game tickets, work on the grounds crew, be part of the team call center, sell team items, sell food at games, teach lessons, sell sports memorabilia.
- **YouTube Channel:** yoga, makeup, hair, cooking, custom designs, entertaining, stock picking — whatever your interest is you can make videos and educate others via a YouTube online channel.
- **Music:** play in a band, sing, teach music lessons, sell instruments, be a voice teacher, work at a radio station.
- **Crafts:** make and sell any kind of craft online and/or at community markets, flea markets, and festivals (e.g., jewelry, pottery, blown glass, paintings, hand-

made art, hair bows, knitted sweaters, scarves).

- **Antiques:** buy and sell, work in an antiques shop.
- **Sewing:** make items and sell at community fairs or farmers' markets, sell items online at Etsy or eBay, do alterations, make and sell costumes for pets.

Here are more specifically income-earning options:

■ **Retail clerk:** 29% of HR managers from large national retail stores say they plan to hire retirees.

■ **Personal assistant:** You might be able to use your skills to help a family by being an assistant who does just about everything from helping with household chores to addressing Christmas cards, shopping to driving children, or anything else the family or professional needs you to do.

■ **Kids' chauffeur:** This is a position where you can make some extra money and really feel like you're part of a family. You become the nanny or "manny" whose responsibilities include picking up the kids from school and driving them to activities — music les-

sons, sports practices, tutoring appointments, etc. — and then taking them home
and remaining with them until a parent gets
there.

■ **Tour guide:** Museums, duck boats,
wineries, historical sites, aquariums, city
tours, any places a tourist might go often
need tour guides. This is a great job if you
love meeting new people.

■ **Driver:** Uber or Lyft! You use your own
car and work whenever you want to. An easy
way to make a little extra cash driving
people where they need to go. Many elderly
people need (and pay) a driver to take them
to the doctor or grocery store. Ask around,
as these will likely be networked jobs. Your
driving skills might also be put to work in a
limo or school bus or airport shuttle — all
services looking for drivers.

■ **Sports:** Love sports? Many seasonal
workers are hired by professional teams and
for college sporting events and team operations. Jobs such as selling tickets, being an
usher, selling food, working maintenance,
etc. Check the team or college athletics
websites for seasonal job openings.

■ **Work-from-home call centers:** A lot of people take on a position where they're paid to sit at home, by the computer, and answer their telephone, to offer information to callers. Not bad because you can sit in your pajamas and still do the job.

■ **Tutor:** Whether online or at a retail storefront offering tutoring, this is a great opportunity to help students while you earn a nice salary for every hour worked. Or you advertise at the local school and do tutoring in your own home or at the local library. Send an e-mail to the guidance counselors and elementary school teachers telling them that you're available and giving your contact info and background. You'll get busy very fast. Set up a PayPal account to make it easy to get paid, unless you only take checks or cash.

■ **Handyman:** If you can fix things, you will be popular in any neighborhood. Your word-of-mouth reputation will spread like wildfire as long as you do a good job.

■ **Mystery shopper:** If you like to give your opinion, there are a lot of retail stores and restaurants that like to hire mystery shoppers to go in and experience their operations. They want you to have a customer experience, interacting with their staff anonymously, then write a report rating the experience. This doesn't pay a lot, but it sure is a fun job that people have told me they really enjoy doing.

■ **Be a seller:** If you have things to sell, eBay and Etsy are great options. Many bargain hunters go to garage sales and flea markets and then turn around and sell their finds for a nice profit on eBay. Creative people can sell everything from jewelry, hats, scarves, and custom baby items to blown glass and so much more. Etsy.com is the premier site for people who want to buy custom, handmade, or one-of-a-kind items.

■ **Substitute teacher:** Check into the laws for substitutes in your area for both public and private schools. You may only need to have a college degree and not be a certified teacher. Subs can make between one hundred and two hundred dollars a day. And you have enormous flexibility — just say no if you don't want to work on any day the automatic system calls you to come in.

■ **Run your own business:** You set it up. You define the hours and how hard you work at it. (See chapter 12 for detailed advice on this option.)

Now prioritize your top three hobbies:

1._____
2._____
3._____

As you consider your future, be aware of one trap: it is easy to slip into watching a lot of TV. Individuals born between 1946 and 1964 — that's right, the baby boomers — grew up with TV. Most of us have multiple TV sets in our homes. Some people have the TV on nearly all the time, for the noise and companionship. Many watch the continuous DIY, house remodeling, or cooking show channels. It's one thing to watch a few movies and TV shows, but it's easy to slip into a mode of watching too much TV and not socializing and pursuing other hobbies — just something to think about and watch out for.

Most Popular Leisure Activities among Baby Boomers in the United States
- Watching TV: 42%
- Reading books: 40%
- Computer/Internet: 21%
- Spending time with family and friends: 17%
- Walking, jogging, or running: 11%

- Gardening: 11%
- Watching or going to movies: 10%

IGNITE AN OLD PASSION

"As a teen I loved riding my motorcycle. It was such a sense of freedom — a real blast. Then I got in a serious accident, one I cannot remember to this day. I stopped riding after that," says Gary, a retired business owner.

Fast-forward forty years, and Gary is at a charity auction and on impulse makes a "ride the new motorcycle" bid. "I wondered if I still had the itch. Seems I did, because I went out and bought myself a new Harley," Gary explains.

"I heard about a group of local vets who rode, and I hooked up with them. It was five years ago that we discussed taking a road trip. One guy said, 'Let's go to Rolling Thunder in DC' — a nine-hour motorcycle ride away. We expected to be with another nine or ten thousand bikers who were vets or supported vets," says Gary.

Rolling Thunder is celebrated on Memorial Day weekend in Washington, DC. Vets and supporters ride their motorcycles through the city streets in honor of POWs and MIAs.

"When I returned from serving in Vietnam, there was no ticker-tape parade and big thanks for serving the country," says Gary. "We didn't get the respect or gratitude we all deserved. Rolling Thunder is our way of demonstrating we still care about those who died and those who were left behind."

To Gary's astonishment, over one million motorcycle riders were there, united under the motto "We Will Never Forget," in support of fellow soldiers who never came home from war. The streets were lined with visitors cheering and declaring their support.

"It was amazing, unbelievably amazing," exclaims Gary. "I hope to do this forever. If you've never been, never seen this, you truly need to add it to your must-do list and experience it once in your lifetime."

Gary rediscovered a lost interest — motorcycle riding — in his retirement years, at age sixty. He often rides with buddies. Beyond the very special meaning Rolling Thunder has for these men, the camaraderie is addictive.

Do you have a hobby, a lost interest you want to retry? No better time to do it than right now. You never know where it will lead — but likely to finding new friends.

Lost hobby to look into:

_____

CHAPTER 3
WHERE TO LIVE: NEW HOME, TWO HOMES, STAY PUT?

Chase your dream!

When people fantasize about retirement, they often think about their best vacations or how they like to spend their leisure time.

If the number one dream is living by the beach, the number two dream is living on a golf course and enjoying the views, even if you don't play golf. Some think about returning to college and living in a college town and drool over the opportunity to take classes for free (see chapter 11). Then there are some who are simply happy to relax, throw away the alarm clock, and enjoy a nonscheduled life. Many people want their life to have purpose and meaning, so volunteering and making a difference by giving back to society and others is prime on their list. Then there are the creative pursuits, like writing, painting, or mastering a craft that can consume your retired hours. Others need a job — part-time usually — to bring in extra cash. Still others have a hobby they want to spend more time doing, be it gardening, cooking, or pursuing genealogy. And of course many people move to be closer to family.

What do you dream of when you think about your retirement days?

_____

_____

_____

Fantasy and reality may not necessarily match. Obviously your financial situation may dictate how you pursue your dreams, but you can make almost any lifestyle work with good research, ingenuity, and planning.

Ask yourself what you need to do to make that dream into a real lifestyle.

Do you want to be near family? Would that entail a move? Do you like a small town? Maybe you enjoy the activities, culture, and options a larger city offers. Are you thinking about living in a resort area? Being a snowbird? Are you looking for adventure? Do you desire to live in a new country? Maybe a planned living community geared for the active over-fifty-five crowd seems perfect for you. No matter what you choose, you need to plan it and include how you can afford it in that planning.

Where are you going to live? That location, or locations, has a great impact on your Retirement Reinvention plan. You must pay attention to lifestyle choices or options. A conscious choice is better than a flippant "I'll just keep living my life," or "I will just wait and see what comes along," or "My income will dictate what my lifestyle will be."

Your income and lifestyle choices are very interdependent. Too many people fall into "retirement shock," working right to the finish line without a thought to what they will be doing during the next stage of their lives. Maybe they got forced out by a company retirement buyout or layoff. No matter how you end up not working, you need a flexible plan for how to spend the next decade or two or three.

BECOMING SNOWBIRDS

Tim and Sharon left the cold northeastern winters behind right after they retired, and moved to South Carolina, near Myrtle Beach. They had vacationed there and loved the weather and area. Moving, however, proved to be a lonely experience. The good friends who planned to buy a home nearby never materialized (one of them had a heart attack). So Tim and Sharon then decided to buy a motor home and start touring the fifty-eight national parks — a major item on their bucket list. A few days before they were ready to go, Sharon's mom, back in Buffalo, fell and broke her hip. "This event with Mom sent us into a tailspin," Sharon says. "She couldn't stay in her apartment, and she had little savings — a tiny pension and Social Security. When the doctor said she needed rehab and could not live alone anymore, I just assumed my sister, who lived much closer to Mom, would take her in. My sister threw a hissy fit and emphatically declared, no, she would not be a caregiver." So the burden and responsibility fell on Sharon.

She balked at putting her mother in a poor quality nursing home (all Mom could afford). So she brought her mother down to live with them. Mom didn't want to be alone, it turned out, especially at night, so leaving her overnight became out of the question. This ended the couple's dream of touring the national parks, and they now find themselves stuck in a town where they know no one and don't have flexibility to go out and do much.

Dealing with change is hard. Add in the needs of elderly parents, and you need to be a strong couple to survive the family obligations many boomers face.

Betty and Ed took a different approach, and it worked out for them. They had retired from a large health-care organization in the cold northern Midwest and wanted to spend January through April in Florida. Ed was fairly content to do cocktail hour by the pool and play golf, but Betty missed her old job. She felt bored and adrift during their first winter in snowbird country. She found several charities she wanted to volunteer for and was really surprised to find that they did not accept snowbirds as volunteers. Once she returned from her first snowbird experience, she focused on opportunities near her home up north.

"I started volunteering at a cancer charity at home," Betty says, "because I had gone through breast cancer myself." The job was two days a week, and she helped out with event planning, fund-raising, and some marketing tasks. The environment and people were great. It was a terrific experience for Betty. When fall came around, she contacted me about the challenge of finding charity work in Florida. "I tried talking to my coworkers and boss," she explained, "but no one interacted with the Florida office. I sent an e-mail, and the director nicely said, 'We don't use snowbirds at all — ever.' I was bummed out." I advised her to open a discussion with the Michigan charity she currently worked for to see if she could continue her work with them during her months in Florida. I recommended she go to them with a plan of what she could do and how she could make it work. To do this, she should check out different kinds of new technology and apps and create a written plan detailing how she could remain part of the team using Skype and other sharing software. The result: she not only stayed engaged but the group "begged" her to help with a major fund-raising effort that needed a full-year commitment. So Betty now works online and by phone while she enjoys the sunny, warm Florida winters.

Many boomers will move away from the area they currently live in as part of their Retirement Reinvention. Moving quickly can be a serious mistake. Choices about where to live and whether to live in more than one place — and if so for how long each year — must be carefully incorporated into your plan. If you think you may want to move to be near family and grand-children, maybe a dry run, such as renting nearby for a year, is a good way to start. Will the kids be so busy you'll rarely see them? Too many boomers regret the move afterward. Especially if they discover that the kids and grandkids have such a hectic life they have little time for the grand-parents. Other things to think about include how to find work when living in a new place. Or if you split your time, how to have one job or volunteer role while living in two places. Ask yourself how you will create new support networks and friends in a new com-munity. How will it actually be to start completely over?

Whether you move to be close to family, for a better year-round climate, or for a lower cost of living, you will be faced with starting again in a new place. Starting over and having to seek out new friends, places of worship, doctors, and other social con-nections can feel pretty awful. For many, it's a big tsunami that hits after they *have already moved.*

Any fantasy will benefit from a bit of research.

LOOK CLOSELY BEFORE YOU LEAP

Paul and his wife bought a second home, in the desert, right on a golf course. Paul loved playing golf and envisioned spending his winters and summers playing as much as possible. He assumed he'd be able to add onto golf groups and join the winter men's league. Once he got settled in the new house, however, he found out he needed to join the golf club and felt that paying eight thousand dollars a year so he could golf for three months was too steep. "I really didn't know that they'd make me pay exorbitant fees. I assumed they'd have a drop-in or snowbird rate. Big mistake. It seems the club needs the annual money to keep the course going, so it's the same initiation fee whether you play a little or play every day." He could go out to other clubs to play, but it was a major disappointment that his dream of playing out the back door did not work out.

DREAMING OF THE BEACH

"I wanted to be by the beach," explains Jackie, who had retired after a career spent overseeing payments to New York State rehabilitation facilities. "I was burned out by the stress of my job. I just wanted to move away from the cold, snowy winters. I dreamed of going to the beach and walking along the shores every day."

North Carolina was the state the couple settled on. Jackie dreamed of living at the beach where she could go for daily walks. She and her husband, Jim, bought a home five minutes from the beach. A nice, large property separated from their neighbors by several acres. Within a month of retiring, the couple finalized the sale of their upstate New York home and moved down to North Carolina. It took a few months to get settled, but once they were, Jackie found herself bored and lonely. "I underestimated how difficult it would be to start over at age sixty. I had lived in my last community for over two dozen years. I knew everyone in that small town, and they knew me," she says. "Now, I know nobody."

Jackie decided to restart an old hobby and went to estate sales in search of furniture to buy cheaply, then take home and refinish. "This was a fun project," she says. "I worked on a piece of furniture, restored it, and then started another one. After a while, I couldn't keep all the furniture I'd refurbished, so I searched out consignment shops to sell the refinished pieces through. Voilà! A new tiny business was born."

This not only gave Jackie purpose, it also led to her finding new friends. She got to know the consignment shop owners, one of whom introduced her to Susan, who loved finding antique furniture too. On weekends,

Jackie and Susan now go to estate and moving sales together.

"I did get the lifestyle I wanted," Jackie says. "Every morning, my husband and I start off the day walking on the sandy beach for a good, long time. It's why we came to North Carolina, and it's the best way to start our day."

MEXICO AWAITS!

Many baby boomers dream of spending the winter someplace warm. Bill had a fantasy of living in the sunshine and not the dreary rain or gray skies winter often brought. He was a sports medicine trainer, and his wife owned a massage practice and small spa. Bill retired in his early fifties and loved traveling, especially on vacations to Mexico. He and his wife seemed to take longer and longer vacations there — one week growing to two, then three, then a whole month. "We got the idea to maybe go live in Mexico permanently when we saw the ad on San Francisco's Craigslist," he says. Someone was looking for a caretaker in Puerto Vallarta. Well, that was the place where they always wanted to stay on a long-term basis. But since the ad was on Craigslist, they were very skeptical at first. The job was for a couple to look after a fifteen-room mansion that also included a private two-bedroom villa the caretakers would be able to live in for free. The job duties included being around late at night and also doing a bit of cleanup and lending an extra hand whenever a big event was happening, such as a wedding or retreats.

"I had several phone calls with the owner and decided it was all legit, so we flew to Mexico and talked to the owners in person. Everything sounded good. We were able to negotiate and get the three summer months off, since summer is pretty darn hot in Puerto Vallarta, Mexico. It was a big plus to be able to return to the states and enjoy our beautiful summer here in California."

The couple would live for free but pay for their own food. After several months with little really to do, they were asked by the owner to do a little social media and some marketing on behalf of the villa. They were paid a salary for that work. "We loved our experience in Puerto Vallarta. The Mexican culture is amazing. We dreamed of staying during the whole year to experience the many festivals and get into the culture. It's a wonderful place to actually live, and it is an amazing life," Bill reports. "Now, I don't speak Spanish. I have to admit I learned a little and my wife learned a little more, but not very much at all. Yet we were able to get by just fine. We so loved the Mexican people we met.

"Another advantage of being in Puerto Vallarta is that many expatriates, or expats, as we locals call them, live in the area. They always have something going on and things to do and explore. People at home have a wrong conception of life in Mexico. They think Mexico is all lazy times on a beach, lots of crime, and people drinking day and night. I'm not a drinker at all, and most people we meet are not big partyers. After all, this is not a vacation — this is our everyday life. We get to live this beautiful experience day in and day out. My wife and I realize how very lucky we are, because it really is an amazing opportunity to live out our dreams like this," says Bill. Having free rent makes it possible for the couple to live this special lifestyle.

SOME GO NORTH

Many boomers seem to pick up exercising as a hobby — or something they devote more hours to — as a retiree. Couples say they enjoy golf, tennis, hiking, or bicycling together. Swimming is very popular, especially with snowbirds who spend the winter in a warm climate. Water aerobics is fun, and many retirees do it. Dancing catches the ladies' interest — everything from ballroom to Zumba, and even a new one called Nia. Then there are the people who seek out the snow: these retirees chase a different lifestyle altogether.

Deer Valley Resort in Park City, Utah, has lots of retirees who do seasonal work so they can live in a skiing wonderland. The winter brings in plenty of ski-instructor jobs, but the slopes offer options for other work too. Jerry, who retired last June, sold his house in Arizona and moved to the Park City, Utah, area.

"Working as a chairlift guy doesn't pay a ton, but the benefits are great — I can ski for free on my days off!" Jerry says.

This sort of seasonal work seems to be really attractive to baby boomers. There are lots of like-minded folks working at Deer Valley at various jobs that keep the slopes running. It's a win-win for the resort and the baby boomer who chooses this lifestyle. Premium resorts have found retirees are much better suited (and more reliable) than young ski bums for many of these customer-facing jobs. Top resorts like Deer Valley actively advertise for baby boomers to spend their winters there. Some resorts — like Aspen — have housing options, in a dormitory style. Jerry bought a home in Park City, so that wasn't a worry for him. "Places like Aspen are just too ridiculously expensive — even the food is too high," he says. "I love life in Park City and working at the ski resort, and I've actually made a lot of new friends my age. When winter ends, life for me is still good. I go fly-fishing to occupy my time."

WHERE TO LIVE

Many retirees plan to move as soon as they retire — to be near their children and grandchildren, or in a warmer climate, or for a new relaxed lifestyle, or often they just want to downsize in a town or city other than where they currently live.

Doug and Judy left their Seattle-suburb home once their boys went off to college. They moved to a nice beachfront home on the Puget Sound side of the San Juan Islands, about two hours north of Seattle. Accountants, they both got part-time jobs there. They enjoyed the summer and the beach. But as time went on, they had a difficult time adjusting. They weren't meeting many educated people and found it challenging to make new friends. The couple grew to dislike the move they made to this more rural area, and four years later they moved again, to California. Although Palm Springs was nice nine months a year, it was brutal in the summer months. Living in California was expensive, with high state taxes, and they disliked being far from a big city. Their next move took them to the greater Phoenix area, where they built a new home. In ten years they had moved three times, buying and selling homes with each move.

"Moving is very costly," advises Steven, a prominent financial planner, who is often called on to give financial advice. "There are the closing costs on two houses, the repairs to make to sell, the packing and actual moving expenses, and then any remodeling or redecorating you do. Depending on the cost of your home, you can be looking at spending a lot of money."

In Doug and Judy's case, when they finally sat down with a money manager, they realized that moving three times had been a serious misjudgment on their part. The first home sold for $600,000 and cost them $55,000 to sell, figuring in repair, real estate taxes, excise tax, and closing costs. They spent over $100,000 to remodel the northern Washington State home. It didn't appreciate beyond getting *some* of their costs back — some but not all. It sold for

$390,000. The California home cost $500,000 and needed some remodeling. They sold it for $600,000 and built a new home that came in around $650,000. In moving, renovations, taxes, and closing and buying three homes in ten years, they had dropped almost $300,000. They couldn't believe the number when they saw it totaled up on paper. But the amount was accurate.

Moving is a costly undertaking. And people often aren't happy once they make that retirement move. They don't realize that settling into a new location is a big adjustment, and it may take years to develop new friends. My best recommendation is this: *get accustomed to being retired first.* Really plan out any move, even if it's fairly local. One town isn't as close to the next town as you think once you move. If you are considering a new area, especially if it is out of the state, rent and test-drive the area before you make the move. With websites like Airbnb you can rent for a month or two and see if you enjoy the new area. Also keep in mind that states like Florida and Arizona are great to escape the winter but are shockingly hot, and can be somewhat miserable in the summer if you haven't experienced the climate firsthand.

No matter how you look at it, owning two homes is a very costly undertaking. You double the everyday items you have, plus there are repairs, landscaping, furnishings, taxes, and upkeep in maintaining both. Be sure owning two homes is a workable part of your retirement plan before you lay your money down.

BEST PLACES

Go to Google and type in "best cities for retirement in America" and you'll find many organizations and sites that offer lists. You may find some of the same places on different lists, and others too. If you envision your retirement as a long-term vacation, you'll probably head for a spot that offers plenty of sunshine and recreation. But when choosing a city for your retirement, you need to know what it offers beyond the beach or golf course. What's the quality of health care? What about the tax rate and cost of living? How bad is the crime?

STATES WITH NO INCOME TAX

Seven US states currently don't have an income tax:
Alaska, Florida, Nevada, South Dakota, Texas, Washington, and Wyoming.

Look at Bankrate.com, and you'll find several places in Florida on their "Best Places for Retirees to Live" list. Along with cities like Charleston, South Carolina; Phoenix, Arizona (and suburbs); the suburbs of Nashville, Tennessee; Arlington, Virginia; and Des Moines, Iowa.

Forbes publishes an annual list. It even likes a few cities that have winter. Its top twenty-five has included several cities in Florida; three in Texas; small towns in North and South Carolina; Phoenix, Arizona, and its suburbs; Athens, Georgia; Bella Vista, Arkansas; Blacksburg, Virginia; Colorado Springs, Colorado; Fargo, North Dakota; Lexington, Kentucky; Boise, Idaho; and Traverse City, Michigan.

And then there are the ever-popular college towns. Boomers are drawn to learning and intellectual stimulation. They are likely to meet more highly educated people in a college town.

Here is a brief list of college towns that often make "best places to live" lists:

- Abilene, Texas (seven colleges)
- Athens (University of Georgia)
- Blacksburg (Virginia Tech)
- Columbia (University of Missouri, Stephens College, Columbia College)

- Corvallis (Oregon State University)
- Ithaca, New York (Cornell University, Ithaca College)
- Lexington (University of Kentucky, Transylvania University)
- Lincoln (University of Nebraska)
- Pittsburgh (University of Pittsburgh, Carnegie Mellon University, Duquesne University, Chatham University)
- San Marcos (Texas State University)
- Walla Walla, Washington (Whitman College, Walla Walla University)

There are many more college towns to consider — this is just a tiny sample. But do your research, and if you think you want to move, maybe try it out for several months or rent for a year to ensure that the move is what you dream it will be.

THE COST OF LIVING ANYWHERE

Effective lifestyle planning takes research, exploration, and foresight. There are a lot of choices. In addition to location-specific concerns, there are matters you will have to take into account no matter where you wind up. Start out with looking at cost-of-living calculators to see what your options are.

For example, I used www.nerdwallet.com/cost-of-living-calculator to consider a move from my Seattle home to Cape Coral–Fort Meyers, Florida. You can type in your income and discover many factors. Here is what I found:

The cost of living is 32% lower in Cape Coral–Fort Myers than in Seattle.
Housing costs 55% less in Cape Coral–Fort Myers.

SAMPLE HOUSING COSTS	SEATTLE	CAPE CORAL–FORT MYERS
Median two-bedroom apartment rent	$2,068/month	$688/month
Median home price (three bedrooms, two baths)	$552,238	$308,791
Monthly mortgage plus interest	$1,888/month	$973/month

Transportation costs 14% less in Cape Coral–Fort Myers.
Food costs 17% less in Cape Coral–Fort Myers.
Health care costs 28% less in Cape Coral–Fort Myers.
Entertainment costs 22% less in Cape Coral–Fort Myers.

Next I looked at my cousin's situation: he

lives in Chicago and says he wants to live in Phoenix, Arizona.

The cost of living is 19% lower in Phoenix than in Chicago.
Housing costs 32% less in Phoenix.

SAMPLE HOUSING COSTS	CHICAGO	PHOENIX
Median two-bedroom apartment rent	$1,500/month	$969/month
Median home price (three bedrooms, two baths)	$454,905	$311,163
Monthly mortgage plus interest	$1,617/month	$1,114/month

Transportation costs 22% less in Phoenix.
Food costs 13% less in Phoenix.
Entertainment costs 14% less in Phoenix.
Health care costs 4% less in Phoenix.

Housing is likely your biggest expense.

Step 1 is to decide where you plan to live.

Stay put. You remain in your home/apartment/condo.

How long:_____

Downsize home. Remain in same town.

Downsize home. Move to new town.
Location:_____

Rent second home in winter or summer.

Location:_____

Buy second home in winter or summer.

Location:_____

Alternative lifestyle. Explain:_____

Step 2 is to define what is most important to you if you move to a new location.

_____

_____
_____

_____

Step 3 is to establish your budget.

_____

Step 4 is to list the top three locations you can afford if you move.

1._____

2._____

3._____

The big caution is to explore moves carefully and completely before taking action.

RESOURCES

Check out our special website to find more housing info, updates, and other "best places to live" lists, cost-of-living calculators, and various alternative housing options. Go to www.MyRetirementReinvention.com/resources.

Chapter 4
$$$$$$: Dealing with Money Issues

What would you do if you weren't afraid?

Many pre-retirees and retirees worry about money. The common concern seems to be: *Do I have enough to retire for my whole life? How much money is enough for me to retire?*

John is a money manager who advises dozens of people about the financial aspect of retirement. He offered his experience in dealing with pre-retirees and those who have gone on to retire. He has served many such clients in his long career and has some sage advice and insight.

First, he warns, "Do not become a miserable retiree" (or as I say, a failed retiree). "These are people who have no real hobby or interest, and upon retirement stay at home and watch TV. Men get super stressed watching the business channels. If the funds they hold plunge twenty points, they start getting really reactive to the negative flow of

TV news and become very paranoid about their future. This is not the way to spend your retirement."

When pre-retirees come in for retirement counseling, he says, one of the first things they ask is:

- What is "the number" I need to have saved in order to retire?

Second question is:

- At what age can I retire?

In fact, John says, two more important questions should be considered:

- How much money do I spend?
- How much money will I be spending in retirement?

One also has to understand the impact of health and health-care costs, which can be a big unknown. How much will it cost you to keep your existing medical insurance until you receive Medicare?

Health definitely has an impact on spending. In your sixties, you are usually healthier, with more energy, and able to do more and likely to spend more. As you move into your seventies, your spending will likely go down. In your eighties, your spending for outside things goes way down, but you will probably pay more for medical expenses or even assisted living if that need arises.

While some people are tightfisted with the dollars after initially retiring, others start spending money too freely. When you first retire, it's not necessarily a wise thing to go buy a second home, which seems to be something that people do because it's always been the dream or they want to have a nicer climate in the winter. As mentioned — and several financial planners I spoke to recommend the same — it is wiser to rent for a year or two in a new location and be certain it is going to work out before you go through the expense and upheaval of buying a second home.

As we saw in the last chapter, where you live or where you want to move is another key factor in your retirement lifestyle. The true cost of living varies greatly across the United States. You may want to be closer to the children, but if the cost of living is really high, as it is, for example, in San Francisco or New York City, you may have to live an hour or two away in order to be able to support yourself in your retirement years.

America's Priciest Cities

New York City
San Francisco
Honolulu
Boston
Washington, DC
Oakland
San Jose
San Diego

A house can be a piggy bank. It's common for folks to decide to downsize and purchase something smaller and less costly now that the kids are gone. If you can free up some money that you can either invest or use to cover the cost of some of the expenses you might have in the first couple of years of retirement, such as travel to places you've always wanted to visit and doing things that you've always had on your bucket list, then that may be the best decision for you. I do recommend you get excellent financial planning advice before you act on any big decisions such as relocation and selling or buying new houses.

Tom, another financial advisor, suggested that you stop paying for your children's expenses once you retire. Many children are in their twenties when their parents get close to retiring and need extra help financially to maintain a decent lifestyle. Some parents will help out by paying some of their kids' rent, especially if they live in an expensive city. It's one thing to pay kids' expenses while you're working, but it's another when you're not. Several financial planners told me that some people keep working simply to cover the cost of paying for their adult children's lifestyle. A good planning strategy would be to cut off the kids, with the exception of birthday gifts, Christmas gifts, and a few baby gifts when a new grandchild comes along.

The Worst Thing Was . . .

"The worst thing we did was remortgage the house to pay for the kids to go to college."

"The worst thing was that I didn't plan and save early enough."

"The worst thing was the vultures swooping in. By this I mean the many, many 'financial advisors' who flooded my e-mail, snail mail, and cell phone with messages about how they could handle my money and make my retirement 'great' from a financial standpoint. The vast majority were sharks — kindest word I can use — and not able to provide the financial security promised. This is something not addressed, and people need to be warned."

"The worst mistake I made was being fully invested in the stock market. This was the biggest one, which I regret immensely Be very careful with investing in the stock market. *In fact, for most people, it's best to avoid it completely. Bottom line: the stock market is like a casino, with similar risks. And no matter how much research and knowledge you gain about investing, the biggest factor in 'making money' in the stock market . . . is —drum roll, please — ta-da:* luck. *Yep . . . plain old luck!"*

BRIDGE JOB VERSUS DAY JOB

You will begin to hear a lot more about "bridge jobs." A bridge job is a transition period from your full-time position during which you are still working but with a set time frame to end your employment. Those most commonly attracted to bridge jobs are workers who are approaching full retirement but are not quite ready to leave. A bridge job can be full- or, preferably, part-time. Bridge jobs will be growing fast in popularity. More companies seem to be willing to accommodate this transition because it is helpful to them to get a new person in place while someone is still there to train them and pass the baton. Typically, this is a four-to six-month process for administrative and professional workers, and up to one year for executives. Some people stay for a couple of years if they can work part-time. Some jobs are better suited to it than others. Obviously some companies are more progressive when it comes to following new HR trends. Don't expect every company to be amenable to this option. Competitive environments and high-tech companies in particular are likely to be resistant. But it never hurts to ask!

Bridge jobs are not typically "offered" by most companies today. It is key to know that HR and bosses are not legally allowed to ask when you plan to retire. You, the employee, will need to go to your manager and HR with a plan outlining how you can train a new hire while stepping back from your job and why it is a plus for the employer too.

Jim is a sixty-eight-year-old distribution program manager whose job involves working with Amazon. Not only is his sixty-hour-a-week position stressful, but he also wants to move away from the congestion, high taxes, and cost of living in a big city. In addition, he has recently had some major health issues. Despite all this, he feels compelled to work until age seventy and is convinced he needs the extra years of salary to add to his retirement savings. He has seen many of his friends leave the workforce at sixty-five only to try to return a year or two later because they say retirement is expensive. The friends feel they don't have enough money. Jim is terrified that he'll run out of money and worries incessantly about not having enough savings to retire. He lost his job at age sixty-two and was unemployed for two years until his former employer called and hired him back. He needs to save more to be able to cover the cost of supporting himself and his wife for another fifteen to twenty years once they both stop working.

In Jim's case, he is making the right decision. He needs to make as much money as he can. If that describes you, definitely do not quit your day job. In Jim's case, his company let him go when they went through a merger. All his efforts to find another job failed. He was lucky that he got called back when the major client he had worked with, Amazon, complained loudly to the new management that they didn't like the new distribution manager and wanted to work with Jim.

He says, "Losing my job caused me and my wife to dip into our savings to get by. I saw how fast the money goes out. And we just haven't saved enough. I wish I could go back in time and really max out my 401(k) and never touch it. I'd be in a lot better shape."

Jim is hoping for another two years making top dollar and trying to save as much as possible. If you find yourself in a situation where you need money to live on, try to stick with your career as long as you can. That's where you'll earn the most income as it is best aligned with your skills.

Helen was planning on retiring at age sixty, when she was blindsided by her husband, who asked for a divorce. A counselor for a clinic, she stayed on for a couple more years because she needed both the medical insurance and the income. She attended my "What's Next, Baby Boomers?" workshop and came up and talked to me about her situation. I made a suggestion that she said made great sense to her. I recommended that she go to her company and suggest she reduce her hours to three days a week (and make sure those hours were enough to maintain her employer-paid health insurance). By remaining part-time, she'd lower her stress and still keep her medical insurance, which she needed until she could get Medicare at age sixty-five.

This kind of transitional period between your career and retirement is what we've been talking about: a bridge job. Helen's talk with her employer went very well. She would stay on, working three full days a week, then retire the day after she turned sixty-five.

My best career advice to anyone contemplating retirement is to try to set up a bridge job. Many people do best transitioning into retirement by working part-time first. Going cold turkey and one day leaving your job after working day in and day out for decades can be very hard. If you're trying to visualize your retirement and you can't see what you'll be doing, you may need to take a year working part-time and develop some new hobbies. A bridge job is an excellent way to ease into your Retirement Reinvention.

If your company doesn't offer part-time or bridge jobs, you can create that option yourself. Start by talking to your boss or HR manager. Share your retirement plans and the last day you plan to work. Discuss how you'd like to create a bridge job and sell the idea that this is a win-win situation. You may be surprised to find that the company loves the idea. As time goes on, this new trend will become more and more popular.

Another way to create a bridge job is to consider developing one for yourself by taking on a role as a consultant or a college instructor. Teaching is an area that attracts many baby boomers. It and consulting allow more say over the hours one works. For boomers who have gone to college, minimal training is needed to move into teaching or consulting, which also makes those jobs attractive.

TEACHING

To get a teaching job, first determine what subject you would teach. Although many college instructors may never have taken a class in how to develop a curriculum and teach a class, you should find one and complete it. These courses are offered by education departments at four-year colleges, and online courses are available too. The time you spend taking this class will save you a lot of headaches. In addition, try to find a mentor or friend who can advise you on this new role. Typically, four-year colleges and universities want people who hold a master's degree or a doctorate. Community colleges and technical schools will accept a four-year degree when seeking out new teachers. Most colleges have you apply to the department chair for a part-time teaching job. At most community colleges, 85% of the faculty is typically part-time.

If you only want a part-time bridge job, then just look around, as many stores and organizations seek part-time workers.

"I heard a radio commercial," says Vikki, "looking for seniors to help seniors. It was a paid position. So I called. Now I work part-time helping out seniors — usually driving them to doctors, grocery stores, banks, or to physical therapy. I feel like I'm doing something really useful, and that makes me happy."

Maybe a part-time job would be ideal for you. There are numerous opportunities for blending a new hobby and a paying job — likely part-time. Indeed, part-time workers are the hardest for employers to find. So keep reading. Many examples are yet to come. If you need to earn some money, that goal can easily be part of your retirement plan.

CONTRACT WORK AND CONSULTING

Many boomers decide they will become consultants. Starting this from scratch is a lot of work. The easiest path into the consulting world is to already have clients to work with. They might be your former company, competitors, or vendors. Read a couple of books on consulting careers. Determine what is fair to charge in your industry. Check out your professional association as a way to meet people who might hire you. Consulting work often has seasons. Ask other consultants in your field about the good working months and the slow ones, so you can prepare.

Annette had been an HR IT specialist for a large energy company. When she retired, at age fifty-nine, her boss begged her to push back the retirement date, as they were in the midst of a major project. Tired of working too many nights and weekends with no extra pay, Annette declined. The company then asked to hire her as a consultant. It was the unpaid overtime that had driven her out, so she took the consulting gig. Annette began getting her pension and for the next six months also worked a forty-hour week, making fifty dollars an hour. The project took eight months, and once it was done, Annette slipped into a bridge job, consulting eight hours a week.

She says, "The consulting work came as a surprise. The good thing is it helped pay for my daughter's expensive wedding. Now that I'm only there two days a week, I want to earn a little more money. So I called some connections, did some networking, and found one more client, who hires me one full day a week. I plan to keep this schedule for a year, until my husband retires. It works great having extra free time. I have a stack of books I'm finally getting to read."

Starting a consulting business was easy for Annette because she already had a client — her former company. If you can bring some clients with you, that is ideal. You must do the research and find out what the average fee is for your consulting area. You'll need to get a written agreement that outlines the number of hours, fee per hour or day, and when payments will be made.

If you have no clients, the marketing efforts will be more intense. Try connecting to people you know on LinkedIn. Former bosses and coworkers first. They know you and your strengths and expertise. Someone may need help and offer a consulting gig.

Contract work is generally offered through staffing or temporary agencies. These can be found in every large city. I had a good, long lunch with my colleague Phil Blair, who runs Manpower in San Diego, Riverside, Las Vegas, and New Mexico. He is the author of *Job Won.* We discussed retirees and how they might land better-paying temp jobs.

"Only about 5% of the 3,800 workers we send to jobs each month are retirees," Phil explained. "I predict this number of retirees will grow significantly over the next decade.

"Many people who come to work at Manpower are looking for permanent work," noted Phil. "Our jobs typically average thirty to forty hours per week. Other agencies might have more part-time positions. The flexibility lies in picking what weeks you wish to work. If you need extra cash for a terrific vacation, you can work five or six weeks and likely make what you need.

"The professionals that are most needed are IT, engineers, and nurses. In fact, nurses are in such demand that they can become a traveling nurse and spend six months here in San Diego in a paid-for, furnished apartment as part of the job. Of course, snowbirds are welcome and can work in two locations, a big plus if you need to earn some money," noted Phil.

Age can be an issue when you are looking for work. "People who show up looking worn out, tired, or cranky aren't good candidates for our employers," said Phil. "The ideal candidate has three characteristics:

- They are personable
- They show energy
- They are authentic

"We watch carefully as a candidate leaves to see if they 'wilt' and if the personality and energy are genuine," explained Phil. "Another skill retirees can sell is that they can mentor others, especially millennials. Note that you have a calming presence when dealing with work problems and remain calm trying to collaborate with others to solve them."

This is sage advice from a CEO who does a major amount of hiring in this growing field.

BUDGET

You will need a realistic budget and to plan for how much money you'll be able to spend in retirement. For many people, the wisest thing to do is to work with a reputable financial planner who can help them understand what their Social Security will pay and how much of their savings they can reasonably spend each month.

Your age when you start taking Social Security has a big impact on the amount you receive each month. In addition, you also need to understand the relationship between Social Security and Medicare. The fact that Social Security is subject to a reduction to pay for your part of the Medicare premiums is unknown to many people planning for retirement. They think that their Social Security paycheck will be what appears on the Social Security Administration report. A low-earning spouse may get up to 50% of the high-earning spouse's full-retirement-age Social Security, but both spouses have the same Medicare reductions before the government cuts your check. That means that the low-earning spouse's benefits get hit extra hard by the Medicare reduction. Also, Medicare premiums have increased at a faster rate than Social Security benefits.

THE MOTLEY FOOL WARNS

When using a retirement-planning program, be sure to figure the net value for Social Security after accounting for Medicare deductions, not the raw number you read on the SSA report. Failure to do so can be terribly misleading about retirement income and the best age to start Social Security, particularly for those with a spouse.

RETIREMENT SPENDING

Household spending declines steadily and dramatically as people age. The expenditures of a household headed by a sixty-five-year-old fall 19% by age seventy-five, 34% by age eighty-five, and 52% by age ninety-eight, reports *Forbes* magazine. This makes sense, as people in their sixties are more active and likely to do more traveling, and to enjoy sports and entertainment, and thus spend more.

When trying to figure out how much money you will need in retirement, the amount you plan to spend is obviously a huge factor. The commonly heard rule is that you will need approximately 80% of your preretirement income to live in the manner to which you were accustomed. The thinking goes that once you retire, you no longer have to make 401(k) or Social Security contributions. Certain costs associated with working — commuting, dry cleaning, eating out — will likely go down, while others, such as health care, will likely go up, although perhaps not immediately.

Money magazine warns that new research on household spending after retirement shows there is no predictable pattern. Yes, on average, household spending shows a slow decline after retirement, but that's because some households spend way less while a considerable number spend more — way more — than they did before retirement. According to this new data from the Employee Benefit Research Institute, almost half of households surveyed (45.9%) spent more in the first two years of retirement. In fact, some seemed to embark on an all-out splurge after they stopped working. Indeed, 28% of households spent more than 120% of what they did in the years just before retirement. By the sixth year of retirement, 23% of households were still spending 120% more, and this pattern held true across all income levels.

What are people spending more on? Housing takes up a bigger percentage of retirees' budgets, as more people maintain rather than pay off their mortgages. A survey of 613,000 households of people age fifty-five and up who use Chase banking services sheds additional light on retirement spending. The results divide retirees into four different spending profiles.

1. The most frugal spend most of their money at food and beverage retailers, places like Walmart and Costco. They have mostly paid off their mortgages and do not have high

property tax bills. In other words, they are the ideal retirees, and likely the model for the 80% income-replacement rate.

2. The next largest category, called "the homebodies," spend a disproportionate amount of income — on average 54% — on various housing expenses, including utilities, maintenance, repairs, mortgage, property taxes, renovations, homeowners insurance, even furniture. These people are living a little too large in their homes and constitute 30% of Chase households age fifty-five to sixty-four and 25% of the group age sixty-five and up.

3. Then there are "the globetrotters," who represent about 7–8% of all households age sixty-five and up and who devote on average 25% of their income to travel.

4. For about 6% of households age sixty-five and older, health-care expenses absorb a significant share of their income, 28% on average.

The report concluded that it seems over-spending happens not on basics such as food or health care but on more discretionary lifestyle choices, such as housing and travel.

EVALUATE YOUR FINANCIAL PICTURE

Getting a true handle on your financial needs and goals will better allow you to make Retirement Reinvention and lifestyle choices. This tool focuses on what you spend. The total output may be higher than what you earn — i.e., credit card debt, mortgage, car loan payments, etc. Looking at your spending, you will be able to see if you have a deficit and what amount you need to earn in retirement to add to and support your retirement lifestyle.

This tool enables you to get a handle on your *current spending* and how that needs to change for *retirement spending.*

FAMILY BUDGET

INCOME

Current annual family
working income $ _____

Current annual family
Social Security income $ _____

Pension income $ _____

Total 401(k)/IRA savings income $ _____

Additional income, rentals $ _____

Investment income $ _____

List: $ _____

MONTHLY EXPENSES	WORKING	RETIRED
Mortgage / rent / HOA dues	$ _____	$ _____
Utilities	$ _____	$ _____
Food	$ _____	$ _____

Taxes	$ ___	$ ___
Clothes	$ ___	$ ___
Hobbies	$ ___	$ ___
Entertainment	$ ___	$ ___
Education / tuition	$ ___	$ ___
Eating out	$ ___	$ ___
Gifts	$ ___	$ ___
Travel / vacations	$ ___	$ ___
Medical expenses / premiums	$ ___	$ ___
Debt payments	$ ___	$ ___
Car payments	$ ___	$ ___
Clubs / memberships	$ ___	$ ___
Liquor / wine, etc.	$ ___	$ ___
Total needed monthly income	$ ___	$ ___

RESOURCES

Find more resources on our special website: www.MyRetirementReinvention.com/resources.

CHAPTER 5
OVERCOMING OBSTACLES

Where there is a want, there is a way.

What is stopping you from going after the life you'd like to live in retirement? Uncertainty? Fear? Feeling stuck? Overly worried or anxious? The reality is that as we age it is sometimes harder to adapt and see new possibilities. Sometimes we do get stuck. Or we find ourselves saying no to new possibilities and options. Below I will outline several types of fears that may hit home. These include being worried about money, having a new 24-7 spouse who is driving you crazy, fear of doing things alone, and being unable to find things to do. I'll discuss each and offer some proven solutions.

There are a lot of "miserable" failed retirees out there. Don't let that be you! Make a plan and act on it. Set some goals. Outline the steps you need to take to achieve a happy retirement. Maybe you aren't exactly there yet. Let's look at a few of the common concerns that often get in the way. Maybe one is an issue for you.

FEARS

Worry that you won't have enough money may be a legitimate fear, or it may just be an uncomfortable feeling that comes with not earning an income anymore. Mike is an investment manager who has worked in the retirement-advising field for over thirty years. "Men have a significant challenge accepting the fact that income is only going out now," he says. "Many people struggle with spending anything at first. They fear they'll run out." He recommends that you make a budget: "That's mission number one. Be cautious of quickly overspending on lavish vacations, boats, or second homes or continuing to support grown children in graduate school or with living expenses. Truth is — no one knows how long you'll live, so you need to be practical and create a livable budget. You are more active in your sixties and will spend much more than you will in your eighties."

Mike warns people to think major decisions through clearly with a financial advisor before running off and, for example, buying a second home. Keeping two places running will definitely drain your finances. He advises people to be careful about downsizing and changing their homes immediately. You should make the adjustment to retirement for a year and then decide on your new living conditions. "Too much change can make anyone crazy," states Mike. "You need time to decide if you plan to move somewhere else. And you must be careful not to lose all the social connections you currently have. Making new friends is hard."

Another solution to consider is looking into finding a part-time job you may want to do. Something where you can make a decent hourly wage and get enough hours to bring in some extra dollars to offset retiring, especially if you have no pension.

"My spouse is driving me nuts." This refrain is often heard when a couple who has never been together 24-7 can no longer seem to get away from each other. How do you navigate differing needs for togetherness, particularly when one member of the couple is not adapting to their postcareer existence? You need to talk about it. And keep in mind that your spouse is not responsible for your happiness. He or she will expect you to develop some independence and activities you don't do together. Ask what activities your spouse wants to do with you — meals, traveling, card games, etc. Then you need to plan around that. Hand your spouse this book. It'll give him or her some guidance to help develop a happier life of their own.

When one becomes widowed or divorced, one is sometimes scared to do things alone. This can also happen when one moves or many of one's friends move away. It becomes difficult to venture out alone. This obstacle can restrict a person's ability to seek out new activities or friends. You need to help yourself by becoming a joiner. Look around for community activities. Consider doing some charity work. Volunteer to help with something important. This will be a solid motivator to get you out of the house. Start inviting others over to do things with you. Invite your neighbors, friends, and couples to your house for potluck. Or invite others to go out to dinner, a musical event, a play, a movie, etc. Make a call today and invite someone to go out and do something this week.

"I live in a small town, and there are no options here for fun retirement activities." This is how one begins to think when one does not think out of the box. Small towns offer their own unique experiences. Even the tiniest towns have community events. People gather for parties, card games, school plays, sporting events, etc. So the answer to this issue lies in what you *want* to do. Look at the goal objectively. Say you want to travel to nearby cities and go to different musical events. Maybe you'd like to go on a wine tasting tour. Maybe you know someone who would like to join you. Ask your friends and see if they know anyone who shares your interests. Maybe you need to start a group.

Lynn was retired and living in a town of forty-six hundred people. She wanted to go to New York City and see Broadway shows. She could not think of anyone who could afford to go, and the thought of flying alone to New York overwhelmed her. She had two choices:

1. Drop the idea.
2. Find a way to make it happen.

As she thought about the idea some more, she contacted an AAA travel rep. She asked if there might be a bus tour that she could take. Indeed, there was, but the company needed twenty people to arrange the trip. The price was reasonable, even if it did mean an eight-hour trip each way. So working with the travel agent, Lynn developed the "Broadway trip." They'd leave on Friday, see two shows on Saturday and Sunday, then return home Monday. Hotel was included, and if twenty people signed up, the price was affordable. Since Lynn was organizing it, she'd get her trip for free. She made up a flyer and an e-mail ad. She posted the flyer at the high school and at the library and grocery stores. She sent e-mails to all her friends and family. On the first weekend in May, thirty-six people climbed onto the bus. Some were retired, some working, a few were couples, plus moms and daughters. And all went to New York City for a big, fun weekend. The trip was a huge success and Lynn now has a job planning three different, special weekends a year to different large cities. She has the bus group discuss the next trip while on the current trip's ride home. She offers some suggestions, and they all vote. She says she has half the group committed to go before they get off the bus, which makes it a lot easier. And it's always very fun.

LOSING MY WORLD

"Work was the center of my universe," confessed Paul, a sixty-eight-year-old product manager, as we sat and had coffee. "The first two years of retirement I had a lot of adjustments to make. My job offered me goals and I was ambitious. I had a focused drive to get it done and felt a sense of accomplishment. Then I retired. No more boss telling me what to do, no more new projects, no more collaborating with colleagues or my team. No more successes. It all was no more. Now you are your own boss and motivator. For me, finding daily motivation has been a big issue to overcome. I can only play so much golf, and I find that much socializing settles around drinking. Cocktail hour at the pool is a daily event that too many retirees see as the day's highlight." I asked Paul why he didn't volunteer, and he said that he was a snowbird and hadn't really thought about volunteering. We spent nearly an hour discussing how a new venture helping others might be a way to stop feeling like a "failed retiree."

Many professionals — doctors, lawyers, CPAs, etc. — have a hard time retiring. Their practice has been the driving force of their life. They invested extra time in training and continuing their education so they could remain current in their field. All that work left little time for much else. Many of the people in this group may be better able to see themselves donating time to their profession once they retire.

Pro bono work — a fancy name for free legal help — is how Jerry donates a few hours each week. The work helped him stay sharp. He had to learn a lot about issues like immigration law — an area he had no experience with prior to retiring. But helping people who come into the county legal aid office has been very rewarding and enjoyable, he says.

Patricia is a physician who donates two afternoons a week to a clinic in the Boston area that offers free health care to low-income women with no insurance. Her malpractice insurance is covered by the agency, and without it she would not be able to do the work. Most of the women served are in the high-risk bracket, so, Patricia says, "It's truly rewarding to help people who really need it."

It was easy for Keith to find a nonprofit that served homeless families. It operated on a shoestring budget and the goodwill of many terrific volunteers. As a CPA, he volunteered to help do their accounting at no charge. He spends one or two days a week at their shelter and gets their books done and handles anything financial that comes in and needs to be taken care of.

A county judge, Eileen found that when

she was working she was just too busy to be able to give much time to anything else. About two years before she retired, she began to get more involved with the national judicial legal association (an offshoot of the American Bar Association) and the international courts organization. She left work at age sixty-five, and is now busy volunteering for these two professional associations. She has worked on committees, chaired a couple, and recently was elected to the board of governors. She's very excited about this, realizing, from a time standpoint, she could never have done it while she was working. Giving back as a national leader is engaging and something that makes her life feel worthwhile. She wanted to remain sharp — a big postretirement objective — and with these volunteer activities, she is.

Bill needed to find a way to give back to his community. He was a dentist before retiring and still lived near a dental college. He did some networking there and was able to get a job one full day a week overseeing student dentists and helping them learn their trade. He loves working with the students, who are excited about the career they have ahead of them. He's also able to advise them about running a dental practice

— something he feels is a major benefit for his students.

I WORRY ABOUT TAKING ON TOO MUCH OF A CAREGIVER ROLE

Many people feel a big tug between caring for their parents or spouse and wanting free time to enjoy their days off. I sure understand these dilemmas, as I have a husband with a chronic health condition and both my parents are elderly — frail but luckily still alive. Let me assure you, if you have elderly parents many issues may lie ahead if you haven't faced them already.

Caregiver roles are hard, because you get pulled between the obligation, need, or desire to help and the fact that the role can be exhausting and feel never-ending.

I saw my mom head into the hospital in serious condition and return home with early onset Alzheimer's. Within one year, she could not live at home with my dad. I had hired caregivers to come in and cook and clean, but my dad hated paying for them to "sit around" too much. Mom went into the hospital again, for stomach surgery, and this time the social worker insisted she could not live at home. So there I was, with them in Florida, and my job, son, and husband back in Seattle. Spending months in Florida wasn't an option. I did move them into an assisted-living center when the social worker insisted we had to. I found it overwhelming, as I had mere days to find an open bed for my mom. It was one of the hardest things to do, as my parents had spent over thirty-five years in their Florida home and loved it. They would stay in Florida with no family close by for several months that year and get only three visitors — one was me. Then my brothers and I spoke to them about a better long-term plan. I moved them to Los Angeles, to be fifteen minutes away from my brother and his saint of a wife, who now helps my parents so much. It's also a much easier trip for me to visit monthly.

Still, they have health issues to manage, finances to oversee, houses to sell, and fifty years of "stuff" that no one wants to dispose of. We used agencies to help with packing and organizing for Goodwill, and hired moving people and a company that did a garage sale for all the other stuff they had in Florida. My dad was certain their furniture and belongings would fetch thousands but instead his check was for about four hundred dollars. Old stuff is old. It may be in terrific condition but it's still old, and often no one wants it.

If you have siblings, you need to talk with them and see who can do what. Maybe one person handles the finances and pays the bills. Another one covers the medical issues. If there is only you, see if a cousin or family friend can provide some help. You may just have to hire people. Tell yourself you are doing the best you can in a bad situation. Believe me, you wish it weren't this way. So do your parents. You'll wish they weren't in a nursing home or assisted-living situation. You'll wish for their younger days and feel sad when you see how old your parents really are.

My best piece of advice for any caretaker is to *set limits*! Think things through and be honest about what you can — and can't or won't — do. Use community resources, siblings, friends, and home health aides to lighten the load. Some of these problems have no easy solution and go way beyond this book's scope. If you are providing full-time care, I suggest you also find a counselor for yourself, so you can work on cultivating some "me time" to offset the demands being placed on you. Be forewarned, you do need to preserve some value in your own life.

VETERAN'S AID

Did you or your parent serve in World War II, the Korean War, the Vietnam War, or in the Persian Gulf War? If they need to be in an assisted-living facility, your parent might qualify for veteran's aid — monthly income from the VA. Start by researching what is available and covered, at www .benefits.va.gov/persona/veteran-elderly .asp.

Anne shared with me why she was still on the job, working full-time: "I'm afraid my parents' needs and my caregiver role will take over my life if I stop working." Anne went on to explain her fear was based in reality. "I just know my brother and sister will expect me to take it *all* over since I devote most weekends now to Mom and Dad, who refuse to leave their own home. My siblings do very little. I can yell at them and complain, but the reality is they won't help much. I'm the oldest, and it's falling on my shoulders."

One wife told me, "I've grown to resent my mother-in-law for stealing so much of my husband's time. He's the only one she wants around and she makes him take her everywhere and do so much for her. She won't move into an assisted-living home. It's making me so mad . . . She's monopolizing our retirement time. It feels like she always comes first."

Laura explained her spouse's health and how it has impacted her retirement and life.

"When I stop and think about what I have done since I retired three years ago, at age sixty-one, it makes me a little sad. . . . All the dreams of traveling, attending all the arts events the city offers, spending more time with friends, volunteering, etc., have been replaced with juggling finances so we can get our son through college without debt, keep up two homes, and being 'the rock' for my husband, who had a career-ending injury in a work accident about five years ago. We are lucky that he survived, but he never worked again after that day. My retirement consists of the two of us going to medical appointments and plowing through operations and other medical procedures. He's so different from before. Living in chronic pain has taken a lot out of him. He hates socializing and making party (small talk) conversations. Three months ago he had his second hip replaced. Believe me — it isn't a terrible life. In fact, I enjoy swimming as my exercise, sunning, and reading a book at the pool. Tonight we are going out to a great seafood restaurant. I think the biggest thing I crave is socialization. I miss the camaraderie that I had at my job. It is harder to come by now when you are retired and your husband is no longer the 'social' person you are. I would say that being a caretaker isn't my first calling, but I do it. I'd advise people to carve 'me time' into their schedule. You'd go kind of crazy, I think, if you didn't."

OVERCOMING YOUR FEARS

Psychological factors can keep you from succeeding at your Retirement Reinvention. Fear can cripple your ability to see and experience a better life during this stage. Whether the fear is of being alone, becoming a burden to your children, losing a loved one, staying healthy, or a deep-rooted concern that retirement represents a path to a scary life phase, recognize that these fears often feel bigger than life. They can cause you to feel paralyzed, incapable, and constantly frustrated. Too often fears restrict us to our comfort zone, and we avoid risks or change that might benefit us.

It's time to take some baby steps to make Retirement Reinvention a realistic and attractive thing. We'll start by taking a big breath. Let it out. Clear your mind. And let go of any negative thought that may enter your head as you consider the opportunity that stands in front of you: having a wonderful retirement. Go outside and pay attention to nature. Go for a walk and really see your surroundings. Walk for at least thirty minutes. Do this daily until you hit one hour. Then walk an hour per day, and your mood will improve.

MOVE FORWARD IN AN EASY, UNFRIGHTENING WAY

I want you to try out one idea, one potential interest or hobby, to get you out of the rut you are stuck in. You might try to find a club or group to join (check out www.meet up.com). By allowing yourself to explore some new hobby or interest — and actually try it — you can and will overcome one of your fears.

If you are truly stuck, have no interests, and cannot foresee what you would do if you retired, then think beyond yourself. That's right. Think about a social or community problem you care about. Maybe it is working on a problem like homelessness or being involved with building a new community park or working with low-income kids. By focusing on helping others, on whom you could support or serve, you can step out of yourself and your fears and make a difference. That is a terrific way to approach Retirement Reinvention.

ALWAYS TEST-DRIVE FIRST

When you do settle on an idea, try it out before making a full commitment. This enables you to learn a bit more about, for example, the inside workings of an organization or a new business idea, a new place to live, or a new organization to join. Test-driving will give you more confidence as you move into something new and increase the chances of success in the long term. Do you like it? Really like it? Yes? Great! You are on your way to improving your retirement. If you don't really like it, if it doesn't feel meaningful or rewarding, quit and look for another opportunity.

LAST RESORT

When I work one-on-one with a client and all my recommendations fail to get that person moving, I know it's time to get some professional help. I recommend that the person talk to a psychological counselor about their fears and the resistance they have to retirement. I also try to assess whether depression is an issue. Depression can be mild but still very debilitating and keep one from living a happier life. If you think you might be depressed, you should see your doctor and discuss your feelings and symptoms. There is no shame in getting a "happy pill," or antidepressant, to get you over the hump. Many older people need antidepressants but are reluctant to ask for help. Don't make that mistake. Talk to your doctor.

TRY IT!

I will caution you that people over sixty can be very good at finding the negative, making an excuse or setting up an obstacle that they've put in their own way. Instead of seeing that a new activity, service, or job could be fun and introduce them to new people and expand their world, they only see what might be wrong with it. You must approach retirement with an "I can do it" attitude. That is imperative. Be open and flexible. Look for opportunities — they are all around if you look for them.

Go back to chapter 2. Look at the long list of hobbies and jobs. This is a starting point that can give you the spark you need to try out something new and different.

SOLUTIONS ARE OUT THERE

No matter what obstacles you foresee or fear will prevent you from having a fun, happy retirement, there are solutions available. Some problems take more creative resourcefulness to solve than others. If you are stumped and we haven't answered your concerns by the end of this book, try asking friends for suggestions. Be open-minded enough to try out some new ideas. You may find the problem is more easily solved than you thought.

Seek out a career counselor and set up a session to discuss your retirement. (Here is a link to my individual client services page: www.MyRetirementReinvention.com/services). A good counselor will help you come up with a plan, solve problems, and find new ideas.

Retirement will happen sooner or later. Let it be on your terms, filled with positive experiences you will enjoy. To do this, you need to tackle any fears you have. Discuss them with a friend or counselor. Open your mind and discover the incredible and fun things others have done as you keep reading through this book. There are so many ideas — many of which you likely hadn't considered. I'm sure something will resonate for you. It is up to you to create the perfect life for yourself. Read on! Others have done it, and you can too.

CHAPTER 6
TRANSITIONING

My survey asked new retirees
what was the first thing they planned
to do once they retired and the
overwhelming majority said,
"Throw away the alarm clock."

Some retirees ease smoothly into retirement, spending more time with hobbies or family and friends. But others, research finds, experience anxiety, depression, and debilitating feelings of loss. A lot of people can go through hell when they retire. They may quietly suffer, too embarrassed or too depressed to say a word about it. Working folks think retirement is "living the good life." The truth is that without a solid plan for how to maintain your happiness it can be a distressing, depressing, and lonely experience. As I have stated in the earlier chapters, people can easily fail at retirement.

RETIREMENT IS NOT
AN EXTENDED VACATION!

Many people seemed to have the misconception that retirement is a holiday. They have spent much of their life being at work, getting to and from work, and thinking about work. The average person works eleven thousand days during their career. The dream of retirement is that it'll be one long vacation. It's not. You will have good days and bad days. Life simply happens that way.

Retirement can be amazing, but you need to prepare for it and work at it like anything else. Anyone who thinks retirement is just lounging around and doing nothing will have an unpleasant surprise waiting for them. Chilling out is nice for a few months, but not for the long term. It's not good for your mental health to be aimless. There are a ton of stories about retirees falling into depression and wishing they hadn't stopped working. You don't want to be a part of that growing trend — do you?

Be open as you transition into retirement. Flexibility and adaptability are two great traits that any retiree needs to incorporate into their ongoing and ever-changing life plan.

But even though life is unpredictable, having what appears to be a good plan for what you'll do with your time *is essential.*

Think back to the other times in your life when you had to make a career change. These are stressful — some are downright difficult. Think about the last career move you made. The time it took to write the résumé, all the effort to find job openings, the networking you hopefully did, then the interview process, and finally salary negotiations — the whole process is stressful. The final stage of your career is Retirement Reinvention. It begins with a transition and the creation of your new life plan. Leaving work for the last time will bring up different feelings depending on how happy or unhappy your work life was. Retirement will be the last phase, and you need to anticipate how making this move will affect you.

If you grew to dislike your job, leaving will likely feel like being released from prison. For most people, however, leaving will bring feelings they might not have anticipated.

Mary Beth was ready to retire, having been a nurse her whole working life, and a rewarding career it had been. Now sixty-four, she says, "I was tired of standing all day — it's hard on me at this age. My son and his wife had my first grandchild and I wanted to spend a lot of time with that baby."

She and her husband had a plan. They would move from Oregon to a new retirement home in Arizona.

"On the day I left my job," Mary Beth explains, "I anticipated feeling happy, carefree, and excited about my future. No more 6:00 a.m. wake ups. No more aching feet from standing for eight hours on hard concrete floors. Time to garden, visit our baby girl, read books, play a bit of golf, lounge by the pool, and relax. I had retirement planned out." But as she headed out the door for the last time, it really hit her. "I just started to sob. I was leaving everything behind — the job I loved, great work friends, even this city. All of it was being left behind. I never anticipated feeling sad, but as tears kept rolling down my face, I was consumed by how very hard it was to say good-bye."

Mary Beth was swept up by one very overwhelming feeling: loss. Something that had meant a lot to her, her job, was now gone. She had told me when we worked together during her career, "I go to work to stamp out disease. It's very important, what I do." Saying good-bye was not the joyous day she thought it would be. She had underestimated the role work and coworkers played in her life. For Mary Beth, her good-bye was final, as she was moving away. That day was a very sad one for her. Even with a plan and things ahead that you really want to do, endings are just that — endings. For many, crossing over into retirement is emotionally painful.

I had anticipated Mary Beth's reaction and advised her to have a family member or good friend from outside work meet with her or even come and drive her home. Indeed, she needed the hugs and support. You may be moving on to something better, but saying good-bye can still carry an emotional wallop. If you think yours will be a sad departure, have someone ready to offer immediate support when you leave. Best that it is not a work friend. Ask someone else who is important in your life — a caring person who you know will just let you feel what you feel.

Even when you do have a plan, as Mary Beth did, a lot of feelings — some sad and hard to handle — can come up. You are moving on, alone, in a big way.

Imagine what it feels like if you don't have a decent plan. Tracy White, chief of human resources at Clark Nuber, an award-winning accounting firm, points out, "I see employees making a big mistake when they avoid retirement planning. Too often the employee just doesn't think about retirement, and that person actually believes that somehow it won't happen. We all know that is not true. Putting a plan in place, one in which you are retiring *to* something, is a much smarter move."

But even with a plan you will likely have some overwhelming feelings on saying good-bye. Many of you will be leaving a life that was yours for decades. You are likely to have strong feelings that need to be acknowledged and dealt with.

LOSS OF YOUR PROFESSIONAL IDENTITY

Mandatory retirement has become rarer. Rob Wheeler, CEO of Clark Nuber, points out that many accounting firms require partners to retire at age sixty-five. Under Federal Aviation Administration rules, pilots for US-based airlines must retire when they hit age sixty-five. It makes no difference how great you are at the job: your professional flying career is done on your sixty-fifth birthday. These people know what's coming and have plenty of time to plan, and yet many struggle with retirement and finding new ways to be happy.

I've had a great deal of experience working with clients who have lost their jobs or ended their working career only to feel depressed and a loss of identity and connections. Some suffer a lot and need to grieve. Some need extra career counseling to move on.

Rob Wheeler notes, "Leaving the job you've devoted your life to can be the hardest transition of all. I know that for me having a Retirement Reinvention plan is the best option. You need to have hobbies and interests outside of work. If you don't, leaving can make you feel lost. I have seen many professionals end up as 'failed retirees.' My advice is that you shouldn't think about what you are leaving behind but what you are going forward to."

As you enter this last career stage, you likely will experience some sense of loss. You are leaving friends and colleagues behind, and for many people, a workplace or organization they have been a part of for a long while and feel a strong sense of connection with.

Others lose their identity. Joe was an executive for a Fortune 500 company and had been there for more than twenty years, quickly moving up the ranks. He held an impressive position as a senior marketing director. He told me, "I found it very hard to retire, but I had come to hate all the travel — and traveling three weeks a month was the job. I realized I would not get another job elsewhere, so I retired. It was hard to adjust, I'll say. I had a lot of influence and felt like I made numerous key contributions to the company. I went from being a 'somebody' to a 'nobody.' When you tell people you 'used to be a marketing director but are now retired,' they kind of think of you as irrelevant. That's what has been so difficult for me. Robin," he added, "I can't really share these feelings with others. They think I've got it easy because I am retired. I've only felt this way once, when I'd lost my job and it took nine months to get hired. Since then, I've been with my company. I'm no longer a mover and shaker — I'm feeling old and like a true has-been."

Obviously Joe has work to do to move on. But a loss of professional identity is a real loss — one you must accept. And you'll likely grieve for a while, but most definitely you have to deal with it.

US News & World Report has stated, "The hardest part of retirement is developing a purpose outside of your job." In the United States, most of us are identified by our job. Often the first question we ask when we meet someone is, "So, what do you do?"

What do you say when you aren't tied to a job anymore?

Without a career, we are left to fill the void ourselves. This is not easy. The UK's Institute of Economic Affairs reported that 40% of retirees suffer from clinical depression. The retirement transition can be abrupt, so it's a good idea to prepare a bit before that day arrives.

It's a question we all face when interacting with people: *So, what do you do?* And it may be a question you dread answering. We tend to measure ourselves by our accomplishments — looking for external validation.

To combat feelings of depression and isolation, try to be around fun people as much as possible. Join an interesting club or group in your area. Identify the one or two people in your life who will cheer you on through this process. Typically, it is not your spouse, who is often too anxious over money and retirement issues.

Many people feel adrift in retirement. Their job gave their life meaning, and not having that is the worst stress of all. That's why some people want to continue to work as long as they can. Individuals who really enjoy their work should try to move into a part-time role (a bridge job) and stay at it as long as possible. At the same time, develop new friends and social connections in your off-hours by joining some clubs and trying new activities you couldn't do while working full-time.

Now is the time to think about all the things you have always wanted to do in life. Is there a trip you want to take? Retirement may be a good time to do it. What were your early interests? Why not volunteer in a related area? Are there friends you always meant to spend more time with? This is a great time in life to reconnect with old friends and make new ones. Think about where you might like to live. If there's a place you always wanted to live but work commitments prohibited it, perhaps a change of location will add to your retirement enjoyment.

RETIREMENT'S PSYCHOLOGICAL ADJUSTMENTS

Too few people consider the psychological transitions that accompany retirement, which can include coping with the loss of your career identity, replacing support networks you had through work, spending more time than ever before with your spouse, and finding new and engaging ways to stay active.

The cultural norm for retirement is that you are living the good life. Truth be told, some folks are very unhappy and downright miserable.

Psychologist Jacquelyn B. James, of the Sloan Center on Aging and Work at Boston College, has found that only those people who are truly engaged in their postretirement activities reap the psychological benefits. That's why people need to invest as much, if not more, time in their social or psychological planning before retirement, to figure out what makes them happy.

Carnegie Mellon University psychologist Sheldon Cohen issued a report that concluded, "Volunteering increases feelings of purpose and meaning in life."

The key distinction I have seen with my clients is that when they volunteer at a place or places where they personally connect, they feel valued and rewarded in using their time to help that particular cause.

PETS HELP

Knowing that some sort of fallout will accompany your retirement can help you better prepare for and plan on ways to help yourself.

The American Pet Product Association says that eighty million US families live with a pet — dogs being most popular (fifty-four million families have a canine pet).

When Tony retired, he says, "The first thing I did was go out and get a second dog. This new puppy was an affectionate fellow. With two dogs, I really have to get out of the house. There is no excuse acceptable not to walk and play with them." The dogs helped him transition and made it all easier for him, as he lives alone. "I get so much love and companionship from my dogs," he says. "They have made what could have been a really rough life transition easier for me, especially now that I have the new puppy to care for and enjoy."

Dogs and cats can help ease the transition into retirement for today's boomer population. Pets provide wonderful companionship and responsibility in what can be a lonely time.

Many retirees have found having a pet inspires conversation with strangers, helps ease the transition from a conversational workplace to living alone, and fills the emptiness created by a less stimulating lifestyle. According to *USA Today*, having a pet encourages increased physical contact. Petting an animal has been linked to lower blood pressure and lower stress levels. Because animals need routine feeding and maintenance, pets provide a sense of normalcy and routine for their owners. Pet owners can often find groups on Facebook or Instagram where people are devoted to (even crazy about) cats and dogs. One retired gentleman takes pictures of his pug dog and shares them on Instagram. He's quite clever and features his dog in all his pictures and has over four hundred thousand followers.

Pet ownership can help you make new friends and join new groups. You might participate in a Paws Walk for a dog charity. We have two West Highland white terriers and belong to a local group of Westie owners. It has events for owners and dogs, and is a fun group and a good way to meet new people.

DECOMPRESSION MAY BE NECESSARY

Anyone coming from a high-pressure, high-demand job will likely need time to decompress and allow those old stresses to fade away and fall by the wayside. The deadlines are gone. The striving is over. Your professional drive may have to cool off a bit. Busy professionals, managers, and executives — anyone who is type A — needs a cooling-off period.

Mysti is a ball of fire. This former executive VP confesses she felt lost when she left her job: "No one was asking my opinion anymore. I wasn't juggling a bunch of balls and getting everything done. I wasn't striving anymore. I'd lost my sense of accomplishment. I realize now how wrapped up I was with my job. I was very good at what I did, and my entire social world was work based. Every workday was jam-packed.

"At first, my retirement felt like a longer vacation," she said. "I went with my sister on a much anticipated five-week trip to Europe. It was absolutely fantastic! Of course I realize I'm lucky; not everyone has the money to travel like I did. So much went into planning and anticipating that trip. When it was over, I felt the letdown, kind of a 'now what?' "

Mysti needed a slower mode, and that would be something new for her. She thought she'd like to see movies and read books. So she got a Netflix membership and binge-watched TV series and movies she'd missed out on before. She started to relax from her usual frenzied pace. She admits, "It wasn't long before I needed a new social group. I'm an outgoing person, but everyone I know is still working. I decided to try out a few things I'd never done before.

Crazy me, I joined not one, but *two* book clubs. I love to read new novels and enjoy sharing my thoughts and opinions about what I've read. Plus, being in two clubs allowed me to instantly meet new ladies, as I'm eager for new friends to do things with."

After a few more months at home, she e-mailed me and said she had joined a gardening club. She also had volunteered and helped raise some money for a worthy cause. At each activity, she sought out people she might like to get to know better. Slowly she made some friends to do things with. She notes, "With all my new clubs and volunteering, I've gotten to meet and be around other people who share my interests. Slowly I'm making some acquaintances I can call and go to lunch with. I enjoy socializing and am grateful I've met some cool ladies in the process of being retired." Mysti is a solid role model of someone who is transitioning well.

You must accept that you will likely have some negative feelings and sadness as you end your day job. Changes and endings are always hard. You can help yourself by exercising daily, having a few supportive friends to talk with, and making a plan so you can begin to engage in a few fun activities.

Decompressing means you let go of the pressures and stresses you faced each working day. You now have no more tight deadlines, no work problems without easy answers. Forget those boring meetings and awkward moments with your boss. No more being forced to be around people you dislike either. As a part of this process, you need to discuss your feelings — good, sad, worried — with trusted friends or your spouse. As you start your Retirement Reinvention phase, allow yourself some time to adjust. You may have been burned-out by work. Or not. Everyone needs some weeks or even months to settle into a new phase. You will need to assess, acknowledge, and accept the changes in your life.

Plan for an adjustment period, the length of which will be defined by you. Several months or up to a year is what some will need to adjust from working life to retired life. New opportunities will present themselves. Decompressing, many say, was key to making themselves into a more successful retiree.

IN PURSUIT OF HAPPINESS

"I was an engineer for my entire career. I worked at only two companies, and I lost my job at age fifty-eight. Since the job market wasn't really interested in hiring an older engineer, I decided to start my retirement," says Dan. At first, he did some long overdue home-improvement projects. "That kept me busy and feeling really productive for a while." But once the "honey do" list was done, he got bored. For months, he moped around. He noticed his wife didn't seem to have this problem; she was always busy and on the go. He asked if he could tag along:

"Honey, let me ride along with you while you do your thing."

"No way, Dan," said his wife. "I don't want you messing up my life. You need to find your own interests and friends."

Her reaction was more typical than not. Couples not accustomed to having a lot of "together time" do not usually welcome such a dramatic change. She might have been open to introducing a new couple activity, had he suggested they take ballroom dancing together or a painting class, but not to just tagging along.

Ultimately, his solution was to join the Rotary.

"You know what?" Dan says. "It's interesting. We meet weekly, and I've made new acquaintances."

Civic organizations like the Rotary often

have a membership of both working professionals and retirees. With chapters in almost every city, you can even attend "makeup" meetings if you travel or spend months in another location. Visiting members (the farther away the better) have a bit of celebrity status, not only in the away club, but within their home club when they return.

In addition to the meetings, a host of committees and events are in need of volunteers. Through the regular encounters, you will make new friends, as happened with Dan.

"One person invited me to join the bowling league. I'd never bowled before, but I went and it was fun. Now I'm a regular on a team," he says.

Dan had to learn to move outside his comfort zone. Trying new things and meeting new people can be awkward, even scary, but ultimately enriching.

MAKE NEW FRIENDS AND RECONNECT WITH THE OLD

Friendships add a lot to your life. As you approach retirement and enter into this stage, you'll see great friends move away. You may move too. A key part of Retirement Reinvention is remaining open and welcoming opportunities to make new friends. So how do you make new friends?

■ **Become a joiner.** You may not be ready for the senior center yet, but look at a community center. If you live in a retirement community, try some of the offered activities. Book clubs are popular. So are card groups and mahjong. Again, there is a terrific online organization called Meetup (www.meetup.com) where you can find a group doing anything you like nearby. If you live near a city, you'll find many groups to choose from. But even small towns have groups that meet to share interests. Cooking, baking, drawing, dancing, and hiking are just some examples. You can find groups for photography, bunco, sewing, yoga, meditation, Reiki, tai chi, knitting, music, sports, writing, languages, and culture — plus, if you have a new idea, you can start your own neighborhood group. Hate the idea of going alone? I suggest you contact the organizer and ask about the best way to break into the group. Maybe make a plan to meet that contact person a little early and ask him or her to introduce you to some folks at the event. That will take the fear out of going to an event where you "know no one."

■ **Facebook** is an ideal way to find and reconnect with old friends. John told me he found several old college and high school friends on Facebook. He says that he found a lot of people who he liked but had dropped out of his life during the busy kid-rearing years. He reconnected and now meets them for lunch, coffee, or to play golf. And he shares his life and family's events on this social media platform so other old friends and faraway cousins can be a part of his life too.

■ **Start something.** Dinner groups, book clubs, movie nights are very popular. Many people would like to join something near their home but aren't one to start something. Why not? Think about a friend or two who might join. Do you have a neighborhood newsletter? A Facebook page? Advertise your idea, interest, or hobby, looking for new members to make up your group. See who responds. I started a book club in my neighborhood with ten people I never knew before. A friend started a sewing group. Clients started knitting groups and poker nights. Don't wait for the group or activity to find you — look for people and invite them to join you. Voilà — you will then have a fun, interesting, and social group of people with whom to share a passion or hobby.

Understanding that your transition time may feel uncomfortable, and setting up some support to help you through, is the best way to deal with this new phase you are entering. Plan your transition now that you know what to expect. That will make it easier, but don't avoid or deny your feelings. Express them by writing in a journal or talking to friends or a counselor.

RESOURCES

Find more resources on our special website: www.MyRetirementReinvention.com/resources.

Summarizing Part 1

We've covered a lot in the first part of this book. You have learned what Retirement Reinvention is about. You've discovered how not to be a "failed retiree." You've read about the myths surrounding retirement and what the new trends are, like having a meaningful part-time job. We discussed hobbies, interests, and the often unanticipated challenges that result from moving from one location to another. Numerous stories illustrated how others are handling retirement challenges. Solutions have been suggested to help deal with fears, concerns, and anything that might stand in the way of creating a meaningful retirement for yourself.

In part 2 we get specific about the things you can do to enrich your life. Again, this includes numerous stories I think you'll find engrossing. Giving back and making a difference in small but valuable ways is covered. As is how to make more friends and enjoy a hobby or two or three. The travel chapter offers some ways to see the world even on a shoestring budget. You'll read about how to take college classes practically for free. Maybe you are inclined to start a business — that is covered too.

Read on so you can uncover the best ways to make your new life full of fun. Whatever you crave, you have to plan it out and provide direction and resources so you can live it. We'll help you do just that.

Dream on!

■ ■ ■ ■

PART 2
WHAT YOU CAN DO

■ ■ ■ ■

Commit to living the best life possible.

CHAPTER 7
WE ALL NEED
SOCIAL CONNECTION

*Let your life be measured by
the happiness in your heart.*

"I was surprised by how much I grieved over losing my work relationships when I retired," says Vera. "It shocked me into realizing that I had left it all behind. I found retiring to be a very *alone* experience."

Some lessons we learn after the fact. In my career counseling practice, many people complain to me that they moved quickly upon retiring and underestimated what a big loss giving up those social connections — friends, neighbors, doctors, churches — would be in their lives. Moving is an all-consuming thing, especially if you are downsizing at the same time. It is also a *hard* thing. You are about to end up somewhere brand new, with no friends or connections. Starting over at age sixty, sixty-five, or seventy is not easy. Don't underestimate the local relationships you have made over the years. Many are pure gold.

"Being an investment banker and living in the world of high finance is sooooo very stressful," says Charlie. "When I reached age fifty-five, retirement sounded like a great idea. I was ready to leave behind the eighty-hour workweeks and to enjoy the good life." After the first year, he was really bored. "I couldn't stand it. I knew I needed to do something new where I dealt with people, but wanted it to be a *no stress* thing. A friend mentioned a young eye doctor who had opened a practice in town and was struggling. He was very competent and well educated in optometry but knew nothing about running a business. My friend arranged for us to meet. We just clicked. I saw a way to be useful — offering business advice plus selling eyeglasses and fitting the doctor's patients for new glasses. It was a no-brainer kind of job, and I get to know lots of people. Seemed perfect for a social guy like me."

What started out as a way to have something to do has been a true blessing to Charlie. He gets to meet so many people who live in the city of eleven thousand people. He loves helping others. But he says the real value showed up two years ago.

"This job saved me," he explains. "My twenty-one-year-old son, Will, was instantly killed in a fiery car crash. He was hit from behind by a man weaving in and out of traffic at 100 mph. That insane driver was high on meth — my son died at the scene after his car flipped, rolled, and burst into flames. That was the worst day of my life. The people I know from my job surrounded me and gave me a lifeline on some very, very dark days. If I hadn't had the job to get up and go to, I don't know if I could have made it through."

Tragedy, unexpected divorce, a major illness — any of life's curveballs — can make you immediately realize how valuable being near caring friends can be.

Marie knew that she needed to make new friends, but she never thought it would be so hard. She watched as her best friend, Ellen, moved away and her other close friend, Joyce, died from cancer in the same year. She'd been friends with those two ladies since her kids were small. They had done so much together, and she hated to admit it — couldn't really tell anyone — but she had a hole in her life. She was lonely but also recognized that it takes a lot of effort to make a new good friend. And *where* would she meet them? How could she find someone who could replace Ellen or Joyce?

Fact is — she can't and she won't. If you've lost your best buddy or good friends have left and moved away, you need to change your thinking. Many people — men and women — are seeking to find a new "best friend." If you are thinking that you can instantly make a new best friend or even make a really good friend quickly, think again. Marie had twenty years of memories and activities in those friendships. You may miss a friend you've known since high school or college. A person like that cannot be quickly replaced. As you retire and move on with this new phase of life, you'll make new *acquaintances.* But deep friendships take time — a lot of time — to develop. You may meet people who over the next ten years can become truly great friends, but it will take a lot of days and experiences together to build that kind of relationship.

As we age, we still want to have a strong social connection to other people. We like to be with people who share an interest. We want new friends to share chitchat about our lives. Yet aging means a lot of people retiring and moving away. You will have to make some effort to get out and meet new people, or you may find your social circle shrinking fast.

Elaine found that her legal practice kept her too busy to do a lot of stuff she enjoyed. After she retired, she wanted to spend more time going to movies. She noticed an AARP piece about movies "for grown-ups." She decided she'd ask a few people if they would be interested in attending the ten best movies on this list and then heading out for coffee to discuss the film afterward. She asked each person to bring a friend and was able to find seven people who agreed to go. Every other week for the next twenty weeks, the group either went to a theater and saw the movie or if it was on cable or Netflix, they went to someone's home. Several films they watched also got nominated for an Oscar, keeping them playing in theaters longer. Elaine says, "I just loved our movie night. These are really cool people who are so interesting. I decided, why not have an Oscar party? I can invite all my new movie friends. I made it an organized potluck. I cooked the main chicken dish and asked others to specifically add to our meal. I assigned one person to bring appetizers, another the salad and bread, and someone else dessert. I wanted it to be a really awesome party, so I told the guests to dress for the red carpet. I was quick to add — wear things you have or items you get from Goodwill to look glam. I personally had a blast running around thrift stores to find a dress, accessories, and shoes. Everyone said the Oscar party was so much fun. I plan to keep hosting one every year from now on."

As for her movie group, it now attends movies every other week throughout the year and has grown to include twelve retirees. Elaine and the others share two things they love — movies and friendship — a nice combination.

TWENTY WAYS TO MAKE NEW FRIENDS

Keep in mind that potential new friends can be older than you or quite a bit younger than you. Both can be interesting and fun to be around. Be open to meeting others, and start conversations with people around you, no matter their age.

1. **Search for a meetup in your area.** If your goal is to find potential new friends, then look into activities you enjoy. Meetup groups are often already established. Go to www.meetup.com and check out

what's available in your area.

2. **Join a church or other place of worship.** Some churches are boring, others are overwhelmingly big, and some are smaller, while others are more friendly. Large churches often have groups within them where you can meet people. A friendly church is likely not too large, maybe fewer than three hundred people, and it will have activities and ways you can volunteer and meet new folks instantaneously.

3. **Volunteer — strategically.** Not all volunteer organizations will fit your needs. If you are giving your time away, be sure you enjoy it. Go with an open mind, but if you go once or twice and that group isn't a good fit for you — keep looking elsewhere.

4. **Work on a political campaign.** You can meet a lot of people, young and old alike, working on a campaign. Maybe you start with someone running for Congress or mayor or your school board. If you believe in their ideas, why not work on their campaign? You'll meet a lot of terrific and interesting people. And

you all have one thing in common
— the candidate.

5. **Join an exercise class or league.**
   Swimming, golf, dance, tai chi, tennis, spinning, yoga — pick something you can commit to doing, and
   do it regularly. Make an effort to
   chat with other people in the class.
   Ask questions if you are new, like
   whether another attendee knows
   about the instructor or how challenging the class is. Anything to get
   a conversation going.

6. **Invite someone to coffee.** You
   have to make the first move here,
   but if you come across a person you
   might want to get to know a tiny
   bit better, take the first step. Everyone hangs out at coffee shops these
   days. It's the perfect way to start a
   new relationship. And, yes, you can
   invite someone without them thinking it's a date or anything.

7. **Find a club.** Love knitting? Books?
   Movies? Biking? Hiking? Photography? Bible study? Cooking? Check
   your local newspapers or with a local librarian about your interest and
   see if there are clubs you can join.
   Can't find one? Start one! Go on

social media and post a notice about your idea. That's exactly how I started my book club.

8. **Take a dance class.** Check out continuing education bulletins from local community colleges and dance clubs. (Google them to find one near you.) Whether you want to learn ballroom dancing, salsa, or just become a bit more comfortable on the dance floor, there are dance instructors out there to help. Many of these organizations have dance parties and even competitions. They can be a lot of fun. You don't need to be a couple to go, so most definitely try it!

9. **Join the Red Hat Society.** As it has over fifty thousand members, you can find ladies to have fun with anywhere you live, even if you live in two places. Emily Yost, the club's marketing director, told me this club is all about having *fun.* They simply join to play. You can connect, via the website, with ladies all over the world and find local chapters and members who live in your community. You must join to see the connections and chapters. I joined

because it looked like too much fun to resist. Each group is different, so check them out and see which one fits your interests.

10. **Take a course.** Colleges offer courses in every subject imaginable. You can take a class on a subject you find interesting but never had time to look into before. Try an English literature course, learn a foreign language, or find out how to do a genealogy. Or take something stimulating like History of Terrorism or art courses or learn more about the environment or take an astronomy class. Try your hand at a writing class. Pick something you want to learn more about. Sign up and start.

11. **Say yes to any invitation.** You meet people if you go to things.

12. **Host a potluck with extra guests.** Decide on a main dish and list the people you know. Invite three, four, or five of them over and tell each one they need to bring a friend with them. This way you'll meet each one of your friends' friends. The host often get invitations in reciprocation for the dinner she or he

hosted. It works for couples or all ladies or all men.

13. **Play cards.** Do you enjoy poker, bridge, blackjack, hearts? Invite a few people over to play cards. Doesn't matter if they know the game — teach it to them.

14. **Throw a party, inviting strangers.** New to a town, street, condo complex, community? To meet the people near you fast, throw an open house or "come meet your neighbors" party. People will come and you'll meet them. Most important, they will all meet you.

15. **Learn to make something.** Ceramics, pottery, a cake, jewelry, glass — try something you've never done before. Groupon offers a lot of really cool activities at a cheap introductory price.

16. **Take an organized trip.** Investigate tours and trips that travel for a service project. You not only get to meet new people; you'll work with them for a week. You will do something meaningful, and you will likely come home with a couple of new buddies too.

17. **Advertise a dog walk.** Find other

dog lovers. They enjoy talking about their dogs too. You can put an ad on Facebook or in a community newsletter and organize a day, time, and location for a dog walk. See who shows up — these are instant friends. Try to find a person to walk your dog with more often.

18. **Join a civic-improvement project.** Contact your local city or town hall and ask about what projects they have coming up. Do they need volunteers? Pick an ongoing project that you can get involved in. This is a great way to meet people in your community.

19. **Organize movie nights (or afternoons).** Like Elaine did, you can pick a theme or vote on upcoming releases. Set up the group so you meet afterward to discuss the film. A local library, for example, often has conference rooms that are free to use — you only need to sign up for them in advance.

20. **Start a new hobby.** Ask around and connect with others who like the same hobby, whether it's going shooting at a firing range, cooking French dishes, or learning to play

chess. A new hobby will lead you to meet new friends.

Check Out What's New
at the Library

I met with Wendy Pender, who holds a unique job within the King County Library System in Seattle. She is the older adults program specialist. I'll admit, I'm not an active library user. I buy the books I read for work or pleasure or for my book club. During my career, I have taught numerous classes on using libraries to search for jobs. So when I heard about Wendy through a colleague, I asked for an introduction. Wow — was she helpful! If you haven't checked out the library, definitely go do so. Besides lending books and e-books, libraries often have great programs to help people over fifty, whether retiring or already retired. For example:

- **Book clubs:** Many different kinds, with different focuses, often meet at the library, as they offer free conference rooms.
- **Friends of the library:** An auxiliary organization that raises funds for the library.

- **Computer skills for people fifty and older:** Volunteer instructors (or librarians) teach computer classes.
- **Genealogy programs:** Personal help and/or courses to trace your family history.

Then there are the newspapers and flyers posted by organizations you might want to get involved with. When I visited Wendy, volunteers were being recruited, for example, to work at the following:

■ **American Cancer Society's Road to Recovery program:** Seeks volunteers who will drive cancer patients to and from medical facilities for treatments. As long as you're willing to devote one afternoon or morning a month, you can be a part of this excellent program.

■ **Chicken Soup Brigade:** Like to chop, cook, or package meals? You can do all these things while helping people with a chronic illness, plus have fun doing it. The soup brigade prepares meals for people in need. This is an opportunity to work with a team of fantastic people who are working to help hungry neighbors.

■ **Habitat for Humanity:** This organization has thirty different volunteer roles for people who want to help support local affordable housing. You can work on construction sites, in a retail store if there's one near you, or with community-outreach efforts. You may also work in the office or partner with the families the new houses are being built for.

■ **Parks and recreation:** Many towns have a parks and recreation center that offers classes to people of all ages. The courses vary widely and might include music, the arts, dance, exercise, as well as numerous other topics and activities, taught by people who just want to share their knowledge. You may be invited to apply to teach. You can also get involved if you want to work on organizing and facilitating the daily activities and setting up rooms, in case you're not a teacher.

■ **Goodwill:** This organization relies on volunteers to achieve its mission of changing lives through offering jobs. There are many ways to get involved, such as supporting job training and education programs, assisting with support services, implementing other important projects, and bringing the fashion collection show and other special events to life.

■ **Food bank:** Seeks volunteers to help fight hunger. You could help in the organization's grocery store, or deliver food to homebound people, or assist with sorting the food that's been donated so it can be distributed quickly to those in need.

Volunteering is the fastest and easiest way to make a new social network or at least be around other people.

List what you could do to make new friends.

_____

_____

_____

Make a goal by choosing a date within two weeks of today when you will try one new group, club, or activity and list the name of the organization here, with the meeting date and time. Also enter it into your calendar.

_____

_____

_____

In summary, if you enjoy others, you will

need to make new acquaintances. They will enable you to have a rich social life, but you must work at it. Take advantage of opportunities to join in. You must be a starter or a joiner — either way allows you to expand your social world as current friends move away. If you find new ways to make new friends, e-mail me so I can share it with others: Robin@RobinRyan.com.

CHAPTER 8
MAKING A DIFFERENCE AND GIVING BACK

What will your legacy be?

The world would be a much better place if every boomer decided to devote five or ten hours a month to working to make society and our planet better. Can you even imagine the impact our generation could have by doing something so potentially world-changing?

Ken and Mary are the ideal pre-retirees. They had a vision of what they wanted retirement to look like. They saw themselves giving back to those less fortunate than themselves. That was their loose plan until their daughter graduated from high school and got a job serving in Africa with Mercy Ships. The organization's four ships are state-of-the-art hospitals that travel to the world's poorest countries and are supported by an exclusively volunteer crew of over one thousand. Why ships? Great question. The

Mercy Ship website states that a ship is the most efficient platform for bringing a state-of-the-art hospital to regions where clean water, electricity, medical facilities, and trained personnel are limited or nonexistent. And because more than 50% of the world's population lives within one hundred miles of the coast, the ships can reach more people who need medical care. In looking for volunteers, the charity asks: "Are you ready to transform lives?" Can you volunteer to help a malnourished baby born with cleft palate, an individual struggling with a disfiguring tumor, or a crippled child? The ship needs medical teams and many other people in various roles.

Touched by the mission of Mercy Ships, Ken and Mary spurred themselves into action. The ships usually require a two- to three-year commitment from volunteers. It is 100% volunteer-based and potential applicants are required to provide or raise their own funds to cover crew fees, insurance, transportation to and from the ship, and personal expenses. After doing some research and talking to a firsthand expert — their daughter, who served on one of the ships — Ken and Mary began saving money and taking courses to better enable them to be accepted to work on the ship once they retired. They wanted to make a difference in a global way, serving the world's neediest individuals, people who would have no health care without this ship's outreach services. This became the plan to kick off their retirement.

After age fifty, we often begin to think about the legacy we will leave behind. We may want to invest in the communities where we, or our children and grand-children, live. We may have knowledge and skills we can teach to children or those who have not had the advantage of our education. There may be an institution, a cause, a social or environmental issue that we are passionate about working on.

In this chapter, you will learn about how to define which cause to invest your time in. You will learn how to "test-drive" before you commit to a particular group or organization, and how to turn your ideas about helping others into action.

Making a difference comes in all shapes and sizes. Some people have a big dream, others wish to do something simpler, but all action devoted to helping others matters.

When we hear about people making a dif-ference, we tend to hear about the big things: stories from the Bill & Melinda Gates Foundation, or how Facebook CEO Mark Zuckerberg is giving away 99% of his Facebook shares — valued at over $45 billion — during his lifetime. These people are making a gigantic difference by donating their wealth to help others.

Here is an amazing story: Muhammad Yunus accomplished what most of us cannot even conceive of, and he began with just a dream of helping people around the world who struggled to make a living. A Bangladeshi social entrepreneur, he started by making microloans to impoverished bamboo weavers who needed to buy tools. Not having any credit, they could not get loans from a bank. Loan sharks, who would have happily advanced them cash, charged outrageous amounts of interest. Yunus wanted to help people living in extreme poverty earn a living and improve their families' lives, and he wasn't about to let their lack of credit stop him. He saw his loans as business-development funds the weavers needed to succeed. He was right: the weavers thrived. To date, he's lent over six billion dollars to more than seven million people, many of them living in remote villages around the world. One small idea about how to help a few people turned into a powerful economic engine that has made a difference in the lives of many. For his invention of and pioneering efforts in microcredit, Muhammad Yunus won the Nobel Peace Prize.

Most of us are not in a position to do what this man did. But that is not important. We each can — and will — make a difference in our own way. Most charities and non-profits need local volunteers. Your neighbors, friends, and relatives are doing things to help others and making a difference in their own ways, usually in their own community, maybe through a church or a non-profit in the area they care about. You can also make a difference and give back to both people and the planet.

LOVE COMES FROM PETS

For people who adore their dogs and want to share them with others, pet therapy is one way to give back. It's gaining popularity with new retirees looking to do something meaningful in their community or at the nursing homes where their parents may live.

In fact, the publisher of this book, Penguin Random House, recently did a fund-raiser for the Good Dog Foundation, whose mission is to ease human suffering and promote recovery from trauma and stress by using

According to the annual *Volunteering and Civic Life in America* report, released by the Corporation for National and Community Service, one in four Americans volunteered through an organization and nearly two-thirds helped their neighbors in 2016, demonstrating that service to others continues to be a priority for millions of Americans.

The organization cited that 62.6 million adults (24.9%) volunteered through an organization in 2016. Altogether, Americans volunteered nearly 7.8 billion hours for the year.

Among generations, Generation X leads, with the highest volunteer rate (28.9%), followed by baby boomers (25.7%).

Source: *www.nationalservice.gov/vcla*

therapy dogs. The dogs work to aid the healing process in humans and enhance their quality of life.

Good Dog provides therapy dog services to people in healthcare, social-service, educational, and community facilities in New York, New Jersey, Connecticut, and

Massachusetts, and at disaster sites around the country. The therapy dogs' work includes anti-bullying programs, working with people who have autism, and helping students develop increased empathy toward animals and each other. Good Dog teams also visit schools and libraries to work with children who are learning how to read. The dogs work in health care and wellness in many areas too. Learn more at thegooddog foundation.org.

A SMILE GETTER

Diane regretted the day she had to put her mom into a nursing home. Mom loved Diane's sweet little all-white Westie, named Spiffy, and she'd beg Diane to bring the dog to see her.

"What started out as just following my mother's wishes has turned into a fun service project for me," notes Diane. "Others may label me as crazy, but I dress up Spiffy in the cutest costumes and outfits and take her not only to see Mom, but also to visit with the other residents in her assisted-living center. The residents and staff love that they can pet and hold the dog. Spiffy is always a big smile getter."

Diane makes sure the dog always has a new outfit when they visit. "They all love discussing the dog's clothes," she reports — dresses, costumes, seasonal getups for holidays (like her red velvet Christmas dress with a beautiful green bow). Spiffy brings smiles and some much-needed joy to the seniors she visits every week. Diane and Spiffy go to two other local assisted-living centers and to Alzheimer's/dementia units too.

The American Kennel Club says therapy dogs like Spiffy are in high demand. Although dogs give us unconditional love, not all dogs are a good fit for therapy work. What makes a good therapy dog? One trained to provide comfort and affection to people in a facility setting. Therapy dogs are not service dogs, which are trained to provide a specific service for a person with special needs.

Therapy dog candidates should be naturally calm, friendly, and affectionate to strangers. They also need to be well trained in basic obedience and able to easily adapt to novel noises, places, smells, and equipment. Therapy dog organizations also require the dogs to be healthy (and to have regular wellness checkups) and be well-groomed, clean, and brushed at the time of all visits. To get started, try the following:

1. Socialize your dog to new people, places, objects, and surfaces.
2. Enroll your dog in a therapy dog class that will prepare you both for therapeutic visits (equipment, situations, handler preparation). Most classes include an evaluation of your dog's potential as a therapy dog at the end of the class.
3. Register with a national therapy dog organization. This is highly recommended as most therapy dog organizations provide support, advice, and insurance.

PRESERVING HISTORY

Mary was a quiet, analytical lady who, until she was fifty-three, had a career doing data processing. By then her kids had graduated and she had the resources to go back to college. She got a graduate degree in library science and then worked for fourteen years as a librarian. She wouldn't have left the job, but the library gave her a fairly big nudge to retire at age sixty-nine, so she did. She had no plans upon retirement and felt lost. A friend invited her to visit a Japanese garden about twenty miles away, for an afternoon, and she was impressed by its beauty. While she was there, she heard that the garden needed volunteers, particularly someone to work in the archive with historical materials about the garden and the family who started it.

Mary says, "I felt strongly that people need to know why this garden is even here. History should be written down." She signed up to become the garden's archivist — developing the collection of historical documents and maintaining that information online.

"I wanted to be in charge of the archives," Mary says. "My volunteer job began by receiving boxes of papers, news clippings, and some information that I needed to make sense of and to recreate the history. I've enjoyed it. The work is meaningful and rewarding. Others will know about this special place and where it came from."

Mary pointed out that many historical nonprofits cannot afford to hire an archivist, so if you like history, detective work, and organizing and piecing things together, work like this might be a good fit for you and your talents.

LENDING A HAND

"I was at a loss when I was not a pilot anymore," explains Larry, who at age sixty was forced to retire from United Airlines because of the FAA and the company's mandatory retirement age. He didn't really do much for the first year or two. One day Christopher Sure, a Kenyan pastor, came to Larry's church and spoke about his community's needs. Larry was moved by Mr. Sure's stories of what life was like in his small African community, Kodera.

"When that pastor told us that 50% of mothers and babies were dying in childbirth, it got my attention. The community had lost three thousand people in three years. And they had no idea why these people were dying."

Christopher Sure asked for the US church's assistance. Kodera is a very remote community with no paved roads or basic hygienic infrastructure and no school or community gathering places.

Larry wondered if he could help. After talking to people in his church, he organized a trip. A group of three doctors and a couple of nurses volunteered to go on the first trip to work with the community. The group arrived and quickly saw numerous issues. The immediate need was to obtain a clean water supply and build artesian wells. Additionally, they needed to teach the people in the community things like the importance of washing their hands and the need for real latrines. Allowing the community to get clean water would solve many serious health issues.

Larry says, "Our American doctors were astounded because they saw things they had only seen in their medical textbooks. There just was so much to do and so many ways we could help." Larry had found his new passion. Over the next sixteen years, Larry and his wife, Priscilla, worked to support this Kenyan community. The first big project was raising money to build a health clinic. On the day the clinic opened, staffed by a Kenyan medical team, one thousand people waited in line. For most, it was the first time they ever received health-care assistance.

Back home, Larry and Priscilla actively raised funds to help support this community. The next goal was to obtain a grant to build a unique elementary school for boys and girls. The community was so poor there was no formal education. So, working collaboratively, the American church raised the money, and the Kenyans did the labor with support from the US team that would come once or twice a year to provide necessary project management, training, and leadership. The children who now attend this new school, Pine Lake Academy, do so via a "sponsorship" system.

Priscilla explains: "A person in the community or church member sponsors one child for a year at the school. That financial donation gets the Kenyan child two meals a day, textbooks, equipment, supplies, and it helps cover the teacher's salary. No administrative money is taken from that donation; it all goes directly to running the school." I was so moved by the endeavor I sponsored a young girl named Frontiah.

In 2006 the school took in its first preschool class. Now more than one hundred students have graduated and gone on to high school. These kids would never have had this educational opportunity without the work that Pricilla and Larry, age seventy-five and eighty-one, respectively, have championed. They remain devoted to continuing to help this cause.

Many places of worship have volunteer opportunities to help others less fortunate. This couple made a difference for a tiny, remote African village. What is your church involved in? Maybe there is a way you can join in and help out, or maybe you can start something, like Larry did.

Baby Needs a Beanie

A retired schoolteacher, Betty used to volunteer in the local hospital every week. Once she hit eighty, she had a harder time standing for longer periods and, regrettably, had to leave that job. She has, however, spent the last eleven years — she is currently ninety-one — knitting hats for the newborn infants in that local hospital.

Betty says: "I have to be productive, and I've always helped others. I love to knit, and I've made a hat for many babies that are the grandchildren of my former students. I knit blue hats for boys and pink beanies for the baby girls. As I don't drive anymore, my daughter delivers the hats to the hospital weekly. This project keeps me busy in a positive and happy way. I can envision that new infant wearing my hat. It means a lot to me that even at my age I can still volunteer and do something worthwhile."

If you can't get out, think about what type of volunteer work you could do from home. You might make things like pillows or clothes, do mailing services for soldiers, put together care packages, etc. There are many needed ways to contribute.

Gerry left the boredom of his couch for work pounding nails and offering leadership skills to build a home for a family. His work with Habitat for Humanity has given his life renewed meaning.

"I was wasting away. I saw the ad for Habitat on TV one day and said to myself, 'I need to check that out. Maybe they are doing something here.' They sure were. Working there and making new friends, as I did, has been a major life-shaping turn-around for me. I'm so glad for this volunteer job that I'm constantly trying to recruit others to come and help on one of our housing projects," he tells me.

Helen, age sixty-three, has an aging mom who, because she has Alzheimer's, is in an assisted-living home. "One day I dropped by, very unexpected," Helen explains. "I discovered the caregivers had chemically subdued my mom and were neglecting her care. Mom stunk from not having had her diaper changed in what must have been hours." Appalled that this could happen, Helen immediately moved her mother. She reported the abuse to governmental agencies, only to learn that abuse of the elderly is a genuine and common problem. That propelled her to start an organization that advocates for the elderly. Helen writes and calls politicians, urging state and federal agencies to more forcibly regulate and help weed out bad elderly care facilities. Frustrated with the meager results, she turned to the media to bring attention to this problem. She wrote articles and opinion pieces for newspapers. She went to her state capitol and has even organized a few demonstrations.

"I've found my mission," Helen says. "I have to stop caregivers from stealing the elderly's medicines and reselling them on the black market. That is happening too much, and the poor, defenseless elder person suffers. Hard to believe this is happening across the United States at nursing and elderly care facilities and homes? Well, it is. My goal is to bring attention to the problem and get it stopped every place I can." Yes, she really is a lady with a mission. Quite a change from the work she did as a systems analyst during her professional career.

Advocating for a cause you care about is a good way to make a difference, especially if you can drum up interest for solving the problem. Helping to preserve the dignity and basic human rights of the elderly will become a larger and growing need as our population ages.

HELP A VETERAN

Walt is a tall man who suffers from nerve pain in his back. He worked for the FAA after his military career, but by age sixty-one the back pain was too severe to work anymore, so he was forced to retire. He was looking for some classes to take to fill up the new retirement hours when he heard about a "friendship program for vets." The program asked volunteers to provide a few hours of companionship a week and to do errands for a disabled or elderly veteran.

Walt contacted this group and signed up for its training program. He found this an easy way to give back and says he loves being helpful. He has become friends with the man he was assigned to, and now Walt tells him to call anytime he needs something. Walt sees this vet two or three times a week, and the vet tells everyone, "Walt is my only friend." What a powerful difference Walt has made in this man's life.

Jean had been her family's seamstress all her life, on top of her other work duties. She made clothes for her two daughters, even their dolls' clothes. With the family grown and gone, she volunteered at the VA hospital in Leavenworth, Kansas, at a shop on the property where veterans can get clothing as they approach discharge. Every Friday, for ten years, Jean has worked in this shop.

She says, "Vets come into the store in serious need of clothing. Of course, many times the donated item doesn't fit properly. So when the pants are too long or other alterations are needed, I tell the vet, 'I'll alter it for you. Come in next Friday and it'll be all done.' " Jean takes the items home and puts her sewing skills to work once again. She does this at no charge. She also enjoys knitting and has made scarf and hat sets to give to the veterans as well.

Jean is really proud to be able to help the vets out. She often tells her two adult daughters about the people she is meeting. On her birthday, holidays, and "just because" days, her two daughters mail her a box of new men's underwear and socks in a variety of sizes with a note explaining, "We know you don't need anything yourself, and these are items rarely donated to the VA hospital shop. We're sure you will see that they find good homes." Not only do her daughters show their support for mom's volunteer work by doing this, but mom gets a chance to brag about her thoughtful daughters when she comes in with a donation of brand-new items.

If someone in your life is volunteering and uses supplies in that work, a care package makes a great gift. Don't know what to buy? Mail a gift card for an appropriate store (Target, Walmart, etc.) with a similar note. It's a great way to support those who are helping others.

There are many opportunities to lend a hand to and show your gratitude to veterans or active servicemen and women.

The mission of the USO is to create a better quality of life for military personnel and their families in the United States and abroad. USO volunteers help with everything from greeting troops as they return from overseas tours and making hot coffee in USO offices to providing warm meals and warm blankets to troops on airport layovers while they're awaiting flights home. Check out volunteers.uso.org.

The Veterans Administration has numerous ways you can volunteer. You can provide transportation, like Walt does; help homeless vets; work on honor deceased vets programs through the VA National Cemetery Administration; and be a part of welcome-home celebrations. Find more info at www.volunteer.va.gov/programs.asp.

BECOME A FAMILY HELPER

Patricia was a very healthy and active sixty-two-year-old who had retired from her job as an administrative specialist working for a large company. Both her children had just finished college and were living in different states. She missed the hubbub of a family. She missed having teens around. She was lonely. Looking at the community paper, she saw an ad for a part-time personal assistant to help out a family. The family needed someone to be the "mom" as the wife was a busy executive and single parent: someone to cook, do laundry, walk the dog, and pick up the ten-year-old son and drive him to his sports activities. Patricia applied and was very enthusiastic in the interview — she wanted to help. The job became hers and for nearly two years she was part of a family again. She loved every second. Then her husband retired, and they moved away. Helping that family had given her a real boost in her retirement. She was sad to say good-bye but was grateful for being needed — it had enriched her life in so many ways.

You would be amazed how often families need help with getting the kids picked up at school and cared for until the parents get home from work. A lot of the job is driving the kids to activities and helping out with the family chores. Networking is the main way to get this job. Also look at the free newspapers you might get at your home with local news inside. Inquire on neighborhood Facebook pages. Check with your local pastor, who is often told about job openings. Contact elementary school secretaries, who also often know about these types of job opportunities.

DRIVERS NEEDED

Before Rick retired from his manager position at the EPA, he started working on Saturdays, when he could, in a program his church ran, helping low-income or elderly people. Since he only had an occasional day to offer, the work consisted of doing errands, getting groceries, and shoveling snow. Now that he is retired, he volunteers two to three days a week and says a lot of the work is taking people to medical appointments and picking up prescriptions for them.

"I just want to be useful, and I have a soft heart for helping out people in need. This job is flexible, and I meet a lot of interesting people in the course of doing this work. It's quite rewarding," says Rick.

Making a difference means as much to the giver as it does to those who receive. Every person I talked to said they received a lot more than they gave. You don't need a formal job opening to help out. Do you have elderly neighbors or older people at your place of worship? Offer a helping hand — rides to the doctor and medicine refills are much needed, as Rick found out.

TOUR TIME

"I'm very proud of my Chinese heritage," said Li Na, a refined Chinese American woman who worked in the high-tech world of Silicon Valley. Her parents only spoke Mandarin, so she is fluent both in it and in English. Upon retirement, she decided she wanted to do something with her culture and found the Chinese Culture Center was the ideal place. She explains, "It is a San Francisco showplace of events, especially the arts. I volunteer and give educational talks to school children who come to learn more about China — its history, culture, and people. We get people who come from all over the world. So I am always on call to conduct tours and educational workshops for groups speaking Mandarin Chinese."

There are so many museums and historical centers throughout the United States that would love to have you volunteer to give tours. What place nearby would you be proud to tell others about?

Bill went online to find something new to do with his grandson. He bought tickets for a Boston duck boat tour, and the two enjoyed the afternoon adventure. Bill struck up a conversation with the tour director. Those few extra minutes enabled him to learn about a cool job — being the tour guide on a duck boat. Bill had been an MBTA bus driver and was bored sitting at home. He listened intently and thought this might be a great retirement gig for himself. They needed extra drivers from May through October. The job sounded fine, so he filled out an application.

"I love my job as a tour guide. Telling the tourists about Boston's favorite sights and a bit of history is just plain fun. I make a few bucks too," he says. The job pays twenty dollars an hour, but, he says, "The tips are really decent and I meet so many people from all over the world. This a great part-time job."

Guiding tours is a fun job if you have a good memory and love sharing information with people. Look around to see where you might apply if you think this is a way you'd enjoy entertaining and educating others.

TAKE FLIGHT

An ironworker all his life, Buck was sixty-three when he retired from his city job. When he was young, he had been a pilot of a small seaplane, an interest that was displaced by work, family, and lack of time. After he retired, he started to think about flying. He read books and magazines to get up-to-date with what was happening in the aviation industry. He was very lucky because he lived in the Seattle area, near the Museum of Flight, and would often go to the museum to listen to speakers and check out the exhibits.

"I was seventy-two when I joined the board for the chapter of Friends of the American Fighter Aces Association. This was a group honoring fighter pilots who had shot down at least five enemy aircraft in World War I, World War II, the Korean War, and the Vietnam War. Only 1,450 aces have ever existed," he says. "As I read and study about them, I find it fascinating," he notes.

"I'm a quiet man with no interest in speaking in front of people, simply because I'm too afraid," Buck explains. "When I was young I tried to do it and just couldn't get up the nerve to talk in front of a small group. Once I retired, I decided to take a course that would teach me how to speak in front of groups. I was interested in becoming a docent for the Museum of Flight. That's what motivated me to overcome my anxiety about speaking in public — the desire to do that job."

Buck took the public-speaking course and joined a Toastmasters group, so he could work on his presentation skills. This solved the problem.

He then began the process of applying to be a docent. A person who acts as a guide in a museum, gallery, or zoo is often called a docent. It's typically a volunteer job. For the Museum of Flight, Buck would talk about a topic of interest, creating his own sixty- to ninety-minute-long presentations. In his case it was a very complicated application process, taking three months of effort, including memorizing a presentation and having to give it before the committee perfectly, with no notes, before being allowed to talk to any guests who came into the museum.

Buck says, "I'm the oldest guy here. What propelled me on is that you get to pick your own favorite topic and talk about it. I did tons of research. I love to learn, and that's what you need to do this. I had to come up with all the facts and information myself and then actually create a speech. It wasn't easy, but I felt it was pretty important."

For the last three years, Buck has been a docent at the museum, offering speeches every Friday. It's a volunteer job.

"This work will keep your brain really active," he says. "I'm expected to continually learn new material. Plus the people I meet — woo-hoo! There was the ninety-year-old man who helped design the Hubble telescope, Bob Alexander. And I'm superproud to say that I have personally met twenty-one astronauts. I sure was most impressed with meeting Jerry Ross, who I've gotten to know rather well. Jerry has spent the most hours walking in space: something like fifty-eight or fifty-nine hours."

When I asked why he took on such a big learning adventure, Buck said, "It's to share with the public. I so enjoy meeting people who come in here. Many come from all over the world. This center is large. We have space camp and a big aviation high school that's part of this organization. The Museum of Flight is designed to educate people. We served 160,000 kids last year. I feel like I'm the least educated person working here. Most of them have master's degrees and PhDs, and I didn't even go to college. I found something that I really loved, and to me it's really making a difference. I enjoy it and look forward to the hours I spend working on this hobby and volunteering."

Buck is a great example of someone who didn't let the fact that he lacked a particular skill or a college degree keep him from doing a job he wanted. He took the courses and spent a lot of time working on developing his skills. You may need to take some courses to get ready to take on the job you want too.

Habla Español

A director of finance, Linda retired at the age of fifty-three. She left her job, after twelve years at the same governmental agency, because she was bored and tired of doing the same things. She took six months off, not sure exactly where she was going, when she met a lady at her gym who spoke only Spanish. "There was something about her," Linda said. "I just really wanted to know her and hear her story." Unfortunately, Linda had only high-school Spanish, and that wasn't enough to make a conversation. She went to the library and checked out a few books and a couple of auditory programs. Then she went online and found a site called Italki.com that matches you with a native-speaking tutor. They have people who speak any language imaginable.

Linda selected a certified tutor. She says the tutor cost about twenty dollars an hour (though you can hire a hobbyist who knows the language extremely well and charges only eight to ten dollars an hour). The company handles the marketing for the tutors, collects the tutoring fees, and then pays the tutors.

"It took me about three years to really learn Spanish so I knew the language inside and out," Linda says. "I did it because it was following something I really enjoyed, and when you're following your heart, you're happy. I just knew I needed to do something that was good in my community and helping people." So now she volunteers at the local library one day a week, working with adult Spanish speakers, teaching them middle-school-level course work. Many adult immigrants from Mexico and Latin America had to drop out of elementary school but now want to pursue more education. They need to do it with someone who can speak their language — in this case, Spanish. Linda tutors individuals on computers and also in math as part of a program called Plaza Comunitaria. She also does sessions for immigrants who want to practice their English with a native speaker.

> About 57 million native Spanish speakers live in the United States today — and another 11.6 million people are bilingual, many of whom are the children of Spanish-speaking immigrants.
>
> Source: *US Census Bureau*

Linda's second volunteer activity also involves Spanish. She works for United Way from January through April as a volunteer helping Spanish speakers do their tax returns. "That," she says, "is a challenge, and it is something I need because I want intellectual stimulation. I need it to survive. My advice to other people is to remain open to the options around you. Think about things you might've done in your past, even in high school, which is where I took my only Spanish classes. Consider everything and anything until something feels so right that you just want to do it every day because it makes you feel rewarded and very happy doing it."

Do you speak a foreign language? Would you like to help immigrants? Check with your local library for opportunities to use your bilingual skills. About 18% of New Yorkers speak Spanish, and New Mexico has the highest Spanish-speaking population, around 47%. The states with the largest groups of Spanish speakers who do not speak English are California, Texas, New Mexico, Arizona, Nevada, Florida, New York, Illinois, and Colorado.

The Eight Most Popular Foreign Languages in the United States

1. Spanish
2. Chinese
3. Tagalog
4. Vietnamese
5. French
6. German
7. Korean
8. Arabic

You might also consider working as a paid tutor through an online service. The largest tutoring service is Wyzant, found at www .wyzant.com.

A DIFFERENT DINNER CLUB

Colleen had just retired from being a senior executive working for a large pharmaceutical company, when she gave herself six months to sit back and decompress from her hard-driven life. No longer on a 24-7 work schedule, she contemplated how she could give back and make a difference. She read a book, *A Path Appears: Transforming Lives, Creating Opportunity,* by *New York Times* columnist Nicholas Kristof and Sheryl WuDunn. As a widow living in California, she decided she'd like to do something where she could meet people. She read about an organization called Dining for Women (www.diningforwomen.org), which really caught her eye.

"This charity is unique in how it raises money. It's a collective-giving model," explains Colleen, "which means although each tiny chapter only gives a small amount, when you add all those chapters' contributions together, the dollars sure add up. Then the organization can make a much bigger difference. This charity works to help women in the most impoverished areas of the world, where some subsist on less than $1.25 a day."

Chapters (small groups) meet on a regular basis — most monthly — and share a meal together, usually in someone's home. Colleen says, "It was easy. I organize a potluck, and everyone brings something to share for the meal. The charity then asks those in attendance to write a check at the end of the night in the amount they would have spent if they'd gone out to dinner. Checks are usually small, averaging about thirty-five dollars. They are written to the charity, and I collect them and send them in. We also spend a brief time discussing the monthly cause or group our dollars will support. Sometimes the national organization sends a video or educational documents or presentations. We can see exactly who we are helping. I think it's an ideal way to combine a social cause with socializing and meeting some very good people."

The Dining for Women website says: "We don't just give money; we invest in futures. The organizations and projects we support educate girls, teach women a skill, help develop markets for their products, and fight the prevalent gender inequality in the world. We give a hand up, not a handout."

Colleen loved the whole concept of funding grassroots projects in health care, agriculture, economic and environmental sustainability, safety and security, leadership, and education. She checked out the membership but found no group in her small city. Her solution? She started a new chapter. She invited a few ladies she thought would like the concept and asked them to each bring a friend. That's how she opened this new avenue to start giving back.

It's great to join in with efforts that are already in place, but you may find that you need to start something, just like Colleen did. Whether it's a charity, group meeting, or community park renovation — you can find like-minded others to join in, spread the word, and help out.

WHEN LIFE GIVES YOU LEMONS, MAKE LEMONADE

"No one was looking for a sixty-two-year-old designer who had worked in the motion picture and TV department of a very large manufacturing company when I was laid off," says Jim. "I looked for another job but all I heard was no. The economy was bad, they didn't want to hire old people, they wanted somebody younger, and I was too expensive. Yeah, I got all the excuses, but what I didn't get was the new job. So I decided it was time to retire and do some things I didn't have time to do before."

Jim enjoyed hiking, and he worked on a major home remodeling project. (FYI, remodeling and other home projects seem to be the first thing men want to do when they retire.)

One spring day Jim went to a park he used to go to as a child. When he got there, he noticed that the rope swing had been taken down — apparently too much of a liability. He sat there and reminisced about his childhood.

"I thought about the rope swing and the fun we had with it when I was a kid. I felt bad that youngsters today were missing out on that." As he mulled, he got the idea that this rope swing might make a good children's book. "I approached this like a major work project. As a designer, I created a storyboard. Then I took a college class on writing children's books. That course should have been called About Getting Published, as we spent more time on that topic than writing. Nonetheless, I took another class on illustrating for children.

"I went to work and created a children's book titled *The Rope Swing.* I did all the illustrations myself and created all the rhymes," Jim says. He didn't think it was possible to go through a regular publisher, so he self-published the book. He gave it to a couple of elementary teacher friends. He asked them to read it to the kids. They did, and teachers and students loved his book. Satisfied, he went ahead and printed five hundred copies and sold them by doing readings at libraries and through word of mouth.

"I did it all for fun, because I so enjoy doing the storytelling part as well as seeing the kids' faces become interested in my book. All the money I made I donated to charity," Jim says. "I had to have something creative to do in my retirement. This has been a real blast for me. I'll probably write another children's book, but right now I'm just trying to think of ways I can sell this one. But, most important, I just enjoy doing the readings and seeing the little faces enjoy the story."

Are you a writer? Do you want to publish a book? Is there a novel in you dying to come out? There are many creative-writing courses out there to try out. I recommend you begin by just writing. You can write about experiences, people you know — anything to get the juices flowing. Then, if a book is really the goal, do your research, because the first thing you need to decide is whether you plan to self-publish or find a real publisher. Once you make that decision, you need to learn everything you can about the option. Talk to authors and learn the pros and cons. Then decide on your subject, create your outline, and get to writing!

Blogs, conversational-style websites run by you (or others), are popular. Is that how you want to write about a subject you love and share your opinions with others? It usually takes quite a while to attract a following, so consistency and patience are key here.

"Opportunities sometimes knock very loudly," says Marcia, who was working for the Social Security Administration as a public affairs specialist. "I had become passionate about issues surrounding women and their money. I was responsible for women's issues, which provided me with the opportunity to attend many financial conferences for women. I also spoke to women's groups about the importance of Social Security and also having pensions and savings to ensure a financially secure retirement.

"I was sailing along when I got moved into a new area, and I was no longer happy or satisfied with my job. I spent a lot of days miserable and thought of retiring, but it just wasn't sensible to retire before I turned fifty-five, which was eight years away. So I kept going to work — miserable and unhappy.

"That went on for a few months," Marcia continues, "and it was one night, crying on the commute home, that I finally decided I was done. So I retired at age forty-seven. Leaving was the best thing I ever did! I opened up a nonprofit called Money Wise Women. And over the next eleven years, I became an event planner — something I've never done before. I would organize conferences about money for women and bring in expert speakers to talk to them. Over the course of the time I had this nonprofit open, we put on seventy conferences in five different states. We did not charge for our conferences. I still get e-mails and letters from women telling me how much learning about how to manage their own money changed their lives. It was very rewarding to know that I was making such a difference."

Last year Marcia held the last conference, and now, at age sixty-one, she's thinking about what her next project is going to be. "It'll surely center on making a difference in the lives of others," she said.

Marcia's story shows that you may find yourself doing something for a long while, and it then runs its course. There is nothing wrong with leaving it behind and moving on. After all, there are so many things *you can do.* If you lose that passion — move on to something else.

FOCUS ON OTHERS

Marilyn and her husband spend one day a week working at the food bank. "Most people would think it's very unrewarding for two high-powered former execs to unpack boxes, sweep floors, help clients get food, and pull all the old food and throw it away. It doesn't sound exciting at all. We both find working here to be very helpful to others," Marilyn says. "We like the people we work with. Most important, I get a wonderful feeling inside when I hand a client a box of food to take home, knowing that at least that person won't go hungry tonight."

Food banks are everywhere. They need a large number of volunteers, and the work is easy but, as Marilyn says, important.

When Deb took early retirement from her administrative job at the factory, she suddenly had a lot of time on her hands and planned to use some of it to help take care of her aging parents. She told me, "The one thing I miss most in my life is being with children. My own two are grown and live far away. I don't have any grandchildren yet. So I was thinking about what I could do. I did some investigating and went to the library to do some research, but I just couldn't seem to think of what might enrich my life." Her friend recommended she consult with me. As we spoke, she said, "I don't know what's available in my area, but

I'd really like to do something with children. I just can't seem to figure out what. I don't have a college degree, so working in the schools is out. Do you have any ideas?" By the end of one session, we had decided that being a substitute aide at her local elementary schools might be a good position to try out. She knew the secretary to the superintendent, because she lives in a very small town. Deb contacted her and filled out the application. Weeks went by. Then she got a call. The secretary said, "Deb, one of our aides is going out on maternity leave. You are the first one I contacted to be a sub. She is the aide to a special-needs child in a regular classroom. Do you think you could do that?"

Thrilled, Deb said yes. She sailed through the interview and landed the job. "I took the job, and it's been incredibly rewarding. I'm making a lot of new friends with the teachers and parents I meet. Some I know, but many I didn't," Deb reports. "I'm really surprised that my retirement is a lot more fun and exciting than my professional life used to be. This new job working with children has really enriched me in ways that I could not have even imagined before I retired."

It may take you a while to figure out what

type of job is a good fit for you. Explore! Do some research and if necessary reach out to a career counselor for a session or two.

A former flight attendant for a major airline, Vicky was a very elegant sixty-two-year-old who no longer worked. She had a big heart and even while working and raising her son did a lot of volunteering.

"The airline dangled a golden parachute, and it was too good to say no to. But me, I love being extremely busy. If I'm not, I get very unhappy quickly," says Vicky. That meant she had to find some worthy causes and projects to devote her time to. She had done some volunteer work at the hospital guild, raising funds for uncompensated care. She'd worked on numerous fund-raisers for them, including a 5K run and online wine auction, and had even recruited live-auction items for the big annual fund-raising event. "I had never raised money before, but I was really successful getting people to make donations for the hospital's fund," Vicky explains. "It's all just talking to people and networking." Her efforts got her placed on the hospital foundation board. That was a big coup, and also a bigger commitment that involves offering guidance and direction, and it has been rewarding but somewhat time-consuming too. Her response? "I couldn't be happier!"

Every charity, college, and many schools have fund-raisers. They all need volunteers to work behind the scenes. Just pick up the phone and call one. Need a suggestion? Check for the local chapter of these large national charities: Salvation Army, Boys & Girls Clubs of America, Goodwill, World Vision, American Cancer Society, Nature Conservancy, American Red Cross, American Heart Association, Breast Cancer Research Foundation.

Do you listen to NPR? Do you watch PBS? If so then you are probably familiar with their pledge programs. David and his wife always listen to NPR. "We love the NPR station," says David. "That is why we are frequent volunteers for NPR's pledge drive and answering the phones when donors call in. My wife was a sales rep, so she is extra talented at getting callers to up their donation to the next level. The fund-raising chair just loves my wife."

The couple says they enjoy the people they meet from the radio station and the volunteers are great too. Want to help out? It's easy. Find your local NPR or PBS station and go to their volunteer sign-up page, and then show up. Oh yes, you need to answer the phone in a nice customer-service manner too.

OH, THOSE SMILING FACES

Angela was a secretary who enjoyed taking out books from the library — she'd been a reader most of her life. She retired at age sixty-three and was at the library one day, talking to the main librarian, when she noticed a children's circle and somebody reading the kids a story. She said, "I wish I had become a children's librarian. I would love to do that job," pointing to the person reading the book. The librarian told her, "That's a volunteer. You could do that if you wanted to."

So Angela signed up to be a story-time reader. She put a lot of thought into it and for her first assignment picked her book on Thanksgiving and dressed, appropriately, as a Pilgrim. The kids loved that she was in a costume and could act out the story. From that day forward, Angela spent her time going to places like Goodwill and the Salvation Army, looking for costumes to go along with the books she wanted to read to the kids. She always goes in a costume that matches the storyline. "This is the best job ever. I have more fun than they do. I just love acting out and being a real storyteller," she says.

Dan goes to school almost every day from September until the end of May. That's where he volunteers. He's in his early sixties and lives in a wealthy suburb. But that is not where he goes to share his expertise. He picked a poor school district in the city and contacted the science and math teachers via e-mail to see if anyone wanted a smart engineer who could teach, mentor, or tutor kids in math or science. Wow, was he shocked when each teacher *begged* him to come in. He wrote me about his experience.

"Robin, these lower-income schools need the most help because they don't have parental support. You see, most of the kids don't have highly educated parents. I work as a tutor and math helper for the advanced kids. I find I don't have the patience the teacher does for the slow math learners. She was thrilled that I could help her smart kids move ahead. I've found some kids who love math, so I've started a math club. We have thirty-seven members, and we meet every week and I teach advanced math. We are going to enter the state math competition for high schools — the first time this school has ever entered. I also advise 'my kids,' as I refer to them, about work opportunities and colleges. I have helped them with college applications and have had a few go on to get scholarships so they could attend college. I'm only one guy — wish I was ten. I come to this school because here I am truly making a difference. And I think I may have recruited another math helper for the low-level kids. I think nothing I've done has mattered quite like the work I do here as a volunteer retiree."

Dan took his time when he started helping out. He listened to what the teacher needed help with, and what the kids might need help with. He immediately saw that the smarter ones seemed left on their own, as the others needed more teacher assistance. After a month, he asked about helping two or three kids do more advanced work, offering to do the planning and come up with problems from the textbook. Dan was wise to get to know the lay of the land and create a good relationship with the teacher at the outset. Once he was certain of what was needed, he made suggestions about how he could best help. The other important thing Dan did was look for a school with a *big* need. Typically, lower-income and rural schools need the most help. They often don't have volunteers. So select carefully so you can make a solid difference, like Dan did.

GET ON BOARD!

Joining nonprofit boards is a very popular retirement job. Lots of women and men I talk to seem to join boards for causes that matter to them personally. Boards need guidance and connections and people with business acumen. Nonprofits get this from people in the community who are willing to donate their time.

Kathy, who has had a lot of experience sitting on nonprofit boards, told me, "I'm very passionate about my causes. I pick them very carefully so my values and goals align with theirs. Knowing that I am making an important difference — that's what really matters."

Many people tout the virtues of their board work, but one caution needs to be put out there. These nonprofits typically want your time and often your *money* too. They expect you to attend the fund-raisers, make a major donation, and also invite all your wealthier happy-to-make-a-financial-donation friends to their events. So keep that in mind and ask the right questions before you sign up, so you clearly know what is expected of you.

Want an active retirement? That is a goal for many retirees. Tom does this by coaching the local middle school basketball team.

It's his favorite sport. His own kids are grown and no longer at home. He misses those days of carting his three boys around. When he heard from a friend that the school needed a basketball coach, he set up a meeting with the athletic director, and for the last six years he has been the team coach, making five hundred dollars a season.

BOWWOWS AND BOOKS

Are you a dog lover? Do you like reading books? Darlene is both. She owns an adorable shih tzu named Ranger. After retiring, she heard about a unique program at her local library, called Bowwows and Books. They have a children's story time and reading program with a unique twist: dogs read with young children. The program is designed to help weak readers improve.

Darlene went to observe the program. "I immediately realized I must do this," she says. She signed up to get her dog into a specialized pet therapy training program. She described how the program works.

"Children come in, ages four to about seven. Typically, these kids are weak readers, the ones struggling in class. Each child selects a book, then picks a dog and owner. While the child might struggle reading to people, they seem to find reading their book to a dog much easier. The owner is there, in the background, to offer a little assistance if the kid gets stuck on a word. Kids read at their own pace, and I find almost everyone wants to pet my Ranger. Typically the kids rotate after about ten minutes. So I'll get four or five different kids visiting and reading to my dog during the story hour."

The program concludes with one owner and their dog reading to the kids. Darlene continues, "I tell the kids my dog *can read.* Then I sit down with Ranger on my lap and begin a story with my dog watching the book. I read out loud and then I command Ranger to turn the page. And he does. The kids scream and get so excited watching my dog 'read.' What they don't know is that the animal is turning the page to get a treat I put on the next page. To them it seems like Ranger is listening and helping turn the page as he 'reads' with me. Kids think this is the coolest thing ever."

Darlene volunteers every week, saying it is a major highlight for both her and Ranger.

COACHING IN PARADISE
Having been a global sales manager for a large company, retiring to Hawaii was all that Patty and her husband talked about. They had bought a small condo years before

and sold it when the market was high. Then, after the market went south, they bought a nicer, bigger one they could spend their winters in, away from Michigan's awful cold and snow. After a few weeks on the island, Patty needed something more important to do. She was a career-counseling client I'd known for years, and she wrote me about her dilemma:

"Robin, I'm suffering from extreme *boredom*! I could not tell anyone else this, except you, because everyone thinks I'm living the good life. They are jealous that I'm in Hawaii and would think I'm crazy if they heard me complain." After all, Patty was living on a tropical island, but she also missed interacting with professionals and coworkers she used to mingle with daily.

We discussed her talents and various options. The most appealing to her was life coaching as a part-time job. She had thought about it a lot. But she didn't want to devote all her time to starting a new business and marketing it. So we came up with a good idea: sales coaching. She had the sales management experience plus was a natural at coaching. She was really excellent at helping others and had done it as part of her career. We developed a plan to launch her new business. She contacted some old colleagues and said she was only helping people with less than five years of work experience. She needed to charge these new professionals something for the coaching, so she decided on a rate of thirty to fifty dollars an hour, knowing that people listen better when they pay. (If she had gone into sales consulting, she could have charged three hundred to four hundred dollars an hour.) She uses technology to "see" her clients: Skype and FaceTime (only on Apple devices). They can also e-mail her if a big issue comes up. They pay her via a PayPal account. She decided to write a blog, for fun, to help sales professionals. Blogging led to more clients. A friend created a small but attractive website for her.

"My clients come from networking with friends and business associates I used to know. My true gold mine was using Linked-In. I found a lot of managers I had known and from them I got potential clients. I have good references and I get referrals. I average eight to ten hours working with clients a week. That's all I want. After all, I enjoy reading by the pool and doing a little bit of painting, which is a new hobby I'm trying out," Patty explains.

Patty has a nice waiting list and usually makes her sales-coaching experience last about six months. It's been the perfect new role for her, and she feels she's giving back by helping new professionals advance in their careers. It's rewarding for both parties. "I feel so needed and valuable. Working with young twentysomethings keeps me sharp and on my toes. It's the best world possible for me."

Is coach a role you want to play? If you have a business background, you can open a business like Patty did or volunteer and still coach others. The Small Business Administration's free mentoring and educational program, SCORE, offers coaching to business owners. The program has more than eleven thousand volunteers, so it's able to deliver services at no charge or at a very low cost. Volunteer mentors share their expertise in sixty-two industries, with free, confidential business coaching available in person or via e-mail. Also, the opportunity exists to teach business workshops (locally) and webinars (online 24-7). Find more info at www.score.org.

BECOME CIVIC-MINDED

Glen worried that his mandatory retirement would be the very worst thing that had ever happened to him. A lower-level manager in a Fortune 500 manufacturing company, he spent over twenty years at the same place and the last ten in the same job. He was angry and then depressed when the company decided that people over fifty-five needed to go. So he lost his job at age fifty-nine, getting only a small retirement package. As the months rolled on, he called me for help. He needed to get out of his funk and wondered if he should look for a new job. After reviewing his needs, and determining how burned-out he was, we spent a session discussing how he could find a worthwhile volunteer position.

"I got to thinking about our career-counseling session as I was driving home," he said. "I saw a poster on my neighbor's lawn for a guy running for the US House of Representatives. I had no idea who he was, so when I got home I Googled him, to see what his views and positions were. They resonated with me. So I took a bold step and knocked on my neighbor's door. I did not know my neighbor, but I asked about the candidate and how they knew him. From that conversation I was invited to 'campaign headquarters,' the candidate's garage. I met the man running and some of the volunteers. I sat down and got to work. I campaigned for months, averaging twenty hours a week. I manned telephones and went out, ringing doorbells and handing out posters and bumper stickers. I did a wide variety of administrative tasks: writing correspondence, handling mail, and assisting in planning events. I really enjoyed this job." Last November, Glen's candidate won. Glen now volunteers at the congressman's local office, doing anything they need.

Do you want to get involved in politics? Start at the local level. Help a potential judge land that job. Or a city council member. You can work on the campaign of someone running for the school board. Getting involved locally allows you to meet new people and quickly make friends with your views and values.

"After three hundred years of teaching English to seventh graders (or was it thirty-five years?), I was tired and ready to retire," says Joy. "I lasted two whole months before my brain went to mush. I cleaned, purged cupboards, shopped until I dropped, tried crossword puzzles — too hard for me — and finally had to admit I was bored!

"I thought I would enjoy sleeping in, but I was no longer tired, so I arose earlier than I ever did when working. I volunteered in my daughter-in-law's classroom, sat in a corner, cutting out shapes, thus putting my master's degree to good use, came dressed as Thing

One and read *The Cat in the Hat,* and never missed a holiday party.

"Finally, I found my calling. I joined a women's service organization, Soroptimist, a group of women working to improve the lives of women and girls with programs leading to social and economic empowerment.

"It was perfect! I was looking for new friends, and I wanted to do some good work.

"Bingo! I have enlarged my friend group many, many times over. There is nothing like the company of good women to support you through the tough times of losing a loved one and to cheer you on with all your good news too. I threw myself completely into the mission: making the world a better place for women and girls through special programs. I joined every committee, made monthly pledges, and gave them my time, talent, and treasure. I became a club president, then one of the directors of our region. I am so proud of the efforts my club has made in helping women and girls, locally and globally. We read to children in after-school programs, assist young at-risk teen girls with career guidance, and offer a hand up to women recovering from drug or alcohol addiction who were incarcerated.

"I am busier than when I worked full-time

as a teacher. My own children often scold me that I am doing too much. My five-year-old grandson always asks me, 'How is Soroptimist going, Grandma?' He has no idea what it is but realizes I am always at some kind of a meeting.

"My social interactions are with fellow Soroptimists now. Many of us are in a book club together, or as I like to say, my drinking club with a reading problem. These brilliant, beautiful women are helping me with my retirement goal: to be just as proud of my efforts in retirement as I was with my career. Retirement is fabulous, and I can recommend it to everyone."

FINDING THE PERFECT VOLUNTEER OPPORTUNITY

You may have your own ideas, but if you don't, let's quickly explore how you can find out about volunteer opportunities. If your local community has a newspaper, you may see some advertised there. But for many of you, heading to the computer is the fastest way to find an answer. Remember that networking and asking others for recommendations can yield better results, but you can get a leg up by combining these efforts and first identifying the job you want online.

Your initial consideration is *where* you want to work — in a brick-and-mortar place, outdoors, or virtual, so you can work from anywhere online.

When exploring, you will find so many different opportunities that it would take two lifetimes to do even half of what's available. I did a brief search myself and found some very unique and interesting options.

Do you like . . .

Horses? Little Bit Therapeutic Riding Center offers a unique approach to therapy, helping children and adults with physical and/or developmental disabilities take weekly therapeutic horseback-riding classes that improve physical health, provide a sense of accomplishment and control, and emphasize the capabilities of each rider.

Forests? Help every Saturday in the spring, removing invasive weeds and dead trees and plants, and gathering broken branches off the ground to make room for new plantings and current trees and native plants to thrive.

Fashion? Thrift stores are looking for weekday volunteers to identify top-quality (and fashion-forward) merchandise from donations, sort donations for use by thrift store and shelter programs, and help move items within the agency.

These are the top causes people volunteer to and financially support, to give you some ideas:

- Welfare
- Child care
- Community organizing
- Education
- Historical preservation
- Health care
- Homelessness prevention
- Women's empowerment
- Stopping domestic abuse
- Disaster relief
- Hunger prevention

Good websites to start your search:

VolunteerMatch (www.volunteermatch .org): This site allows you to find volunteer opportunities wherever you live. It has offered more than twelve million individuals a chance to make a difference by connecting them to nonprofits needing volunteers. **Idealist (www.idealist.org):** With both volunteer and paid opportunities, this site is all about connecting idealists — people who want to do good — with opportunities for action and collaboration. With more than 120,000 organizations and 1.4 million monthly visitors to its English and Spanish (Idealistas.org) sites, this site helps people move from an intention to taking action.

I keep an up-to-date list of websites and other resources. Go to www.MyRetirement Reinvention.com/resources.

CAUTION: TEST-DRIVE!

Not all volunteer jobs will meet your desires or goals. You may try one and find it is not what you thought it would be. If so, gracefully quit. That is correct: I am giving you permission *not* to follow through and instead to leave that volunteer job behind. At first, think of it as a test-drive. If it's great, fully commit. If not, go find great.

Many boomers tell me it took two or three tries until they found the right opportunity. So select with care. Ask good questions regarding the work and what tasks you will be doing so you can decide if it is a good fit for you. Try it out, and only stay if the job makes you feel like you are doing something meaningful.

Think about how you might volunteer and make a difference in the lives of others or benefit our planet. Any boomer who is uncertain how to start a great retirement should give serious consideration to giving back and how to make a difference. You can do something that will help others and make you feel good about doing it.

For more ideas on volunteering go to www.MyRetirementReinvention.com/resources.

CHAPTER 9
LIVE YOUR HOBBY

Embrace your dreams with passion.

An active retirement is a happy retirement. It's a time when you do things you enjoy and want to be doing. You want to keep your mind engaged, your spirit refreshed, and your soul renewed. You want to relax and enjoy activities with interesting people.

Many of my clients enjoyed various hobbies and activities before they retired. Others started after they left their job. The types of hobbies people pursue are many and varied. I, for example, *love* photography and will spend more time pursuing it when I stop working. Other clients have worked on community projects, played in a tennis or golf league, participated in book clubs or dinner groups, undertook creative endeavors or long hikes. The majority of my clients have a hobby or two — or five. Almost everyone says they couldn't spend as much time as they liked at their hobbies when working and they were definitely on the retirement to-do list. Some had an interest but never the time to explore it. Retirement was when they first tried out a new hobby or pursued an interest.

GARDENING IS A VERY POPULAR HOBBY

I love planting flowers and creating a beautiful garden. Others like to plant and grow vegetables. Norma was a busy CPA who was consumed with a very large practice. At age seventy she started to close out her business, and by age seventy-six she had only a handful of clients left. As she was closing this one door, she says, "I knew I needed to open another. I couldn't see retiring if I wasn't doing something worthwhile."

Norma had been a gardener, and at age seventy she decided to join the P-Patch community gardening organization in Seattle. They have a unique organization with the following goals:

- Nurturing civic engagement
- Practicing organic gardening techniques and growing herbs and vegetables
- Improving access to local, organic, and

culturally appropriate food
- Transforming the appearance of and revitalizing neighborhoods
- Feeding the hungry
- Uniting others through gardening and cooking

This group oversees thirty-two acres. Their website says the gardens provide a way to give back to the community. Their gardeners put in over thirty-three thousand hours, supplying fresh organic produce to Seattle food banks and feeding programs.

When the P-Patch coordinator quit, Norma volunteered to take on that role. "I like to organize things. It's something I'm good at," Norma shared with me. "I spend five to eight hours a week on this project. It's mostly run by e-mail. Many of the P-Patch gardeners are retired people. They can't do some of the physical labor on a new or big restoration project, so I'll plan work parties. We get involvement from companies like Microsoft, or from charity groups or high school helpers who come in to do a lot of labor in one weekend or day. The task for me is handling the event planning, coordinating, and keeping our two hundred gardeners organized. You have to be very resourceful and have superb networking skills to do this volunteer position. It's a rewarding undertaking because we can see the results. We create food and beauty. It's a community effort — I really like that. With about one hundred fifty garden plots and more than two hundred gardeners, it has been great fun to keep them all organized." And, yes, Norma does all this at age seventy-nine.

Becoming active in gardening has many options. It's your little spot on the earth to do with as you wish. Getting your hands in the dirt is a good project. I love growing flowers. I was a rose fanatic, but the deer always came in and ate them, so I finally switched to hydrangeas and other blossoms. Look for groups to join on Meetup or join master gardener groups. Sometimes just talking to neighbors and friends who share this hobby is pleasure enough.

BE A TUTOR OR TEACHER

Stephan was a tall, lean, no-nonsense engineer, but at age fifty-eight, he was laid off (along with fifty thousand others). He tried to land a new job, but no one wanted a white-haired, senior engineer who was in his late fifties, very expensive, and looked too old to offer fresh ideas. He couldn't get any work, but he needed to earn a living.

Stephan sadly realized that he would need to do something different. He was sitting around, moping, not able to find a solution to his problem. His brother suggested the idea of being a tutor. Stephan had always tapped into his math and physics skills while on the job. He was good at instructing other workers and had a lot of experience doing it. He checked into this option, tried tutoring, and really enjoyed it. Having never run a business, he found a website to partner with, Wyzant (www.wyzant.com). They advertise for Stephan and bring him clients. They collect the money and take a small cut of his hourly tutoring fee. He gets to meet teenagers and help make the "hard subjects" more understandable for them. He tutors at the local library, making it easier for him to book clients back-to-back.

This new career phase has worked for him. He earns over forty thousand dollars a year, and, most important, he says, the work makes him feel valued and useful. He's got a flexible schedule and his web partner provides a steady stream of potential clients.

There are many subjects to tutor people in. Do you have musical talent? Can you teach piano, saxophone, guitar? What about voice lessons? There are a lot of choir and music leader jobs through churches. If you are good at something, you likely can teach others how to do it. Continuing education departments at community colleges and four-year universities are full of people who teach everything from acting to tai chi to wedding planning. If you have a talent, continuing ed departments and sometimes city parks and recreation centers make great places to sell your knowledge.

RANDOM ACTS OF KINDNESS

"It was after living through a horrible year in which my best friend died and I lost five other close friends that I felt at an all-time low," reveals Marcie. "I was so down and so depressed, filled with grief, sorrow, and heartache. I thought about other people who are suffering through tragedies too. Some have an injury or loss of a loved one; others are going through cancer treatments. I envisioned that, as time dragged on and the initial support waned, they would still be feeling just like I was — down and discouraged.

"One of my hobbies had always been creating handmade cards. I don't know where the idea came from — it just kind of popped into my head — but I thought, what if I was to send a 'sunshine and smiles' handmade card to someone who is going through a very difficult time? I asked around and got the names and addresses of several people who were in need of a card. Then off into the mail my heartfelt treasure was sent, full of sunshine to help brighten their day in a tiny way. This is how I started 'sending sunshine and smiles.' "

Marcie began telling other people about what she was doing. She was at a stamping convention where people use rubber stamps to make cards and told everyone she met. Several people said they would like to help, especially since it was something they could do from home. One year later, Marcie had dozens of people who would message her or tell her about people in need.

"I have several volunteer recruits who will make a card and mail it out. I just e-mail them. This little 'sunshine and smiles' club, as I call it, is performing a random act of kindness — and it works!" Marcie says. Indeed, the club has sent out hundreds of handmade "sunshine and smiles" cards with messages that let the recipients know they're being thought of and cared about or prayed for.

"I love organizing this and we have several people involved now," Marcie explains. "It's a great little community in which we can share graphics along with online photos of the cards we've made. You don't have to do something major to help other people, but you do have to do something. Giving back is the most rewarding thing you'll ever do." That seems to be true based on the e-mails Marcie gets back from people who have received her exquisite cards. She shared a couple of responses:

ES said: "Thanks for the lovely cards. They came at a time when I needed them. It is so nice to know that the Christian community is alive. God bless you and your ministry."

SM wrote: "You certainly have filled my heart with great joy. I have all your beautiful cards together and read them over and over. They brought a smile to my face even on the bad days. I so enjoyed these and think that someone I've never met could make such a difference in my day. Thank you for your kindness and caring."

GK (died of stage-four cancer at age twenty-seven): "The cards I receive from you and your friends have been so uplifting and make you believe in the beauty behind the human spirit. Much love and gratitude to all."

Marcie created Sending Sunshine and Smiles for people who need a pick-me-up. She took her stamping and card-making skills and put them to a wonderful use. That random act of kindness really matters to the recipients.

If you want to make a difference, you have two options:

- Join something that exists
- Start something new

BE A JOINER OR A STARTER

In chapter 2, you identified a few hobbies that might interest you. Now it is time to learn more about the options available in your community.

Begin by Googling your hobby, such as "book clubs" or "hiking," and add your town or city so the search looks like this:

Book Club Parkville Missouri

When you enter queries like this, you'll be surprised to find meetups, library clubs, or community groups that already exist and that you could join.

Another option is to look on your neighborhood Facebook page. Post a question: *Do you know of any local painting groups? Or writing groups? Or cooking groups?* List whatever hobby you seek to find connections to.

A former marine, Bill always went to the shooting range. Once he retired, he moved to Texas. He knew that hunting was popular there, but living in a new place posed a problem. "I wondered if there were any gun and hunting enthusiasts in town and gave some thought to how I would find them. I went down to the Walmart and asked the person in charge of the gun section. That person gave me the names of a few local groups. I made the calls, checked out the groups, and joined the one I liked best. It was easy once I made the calls. I have to admit it took me a few days to call strangers, but I'm really glad I did."

You will likely have to make the effort to find a new group and join in. Meetup groups are springing up all over the United States. As mentioned, Meetup is a terrific online site. You can find others who share your interest or hobby. Like bird watching? You can join a group doing just that. Book clubs, pet groups, writing, sports, photography, cooking, car enthusiasts, over-fifty singles, over-fifty married, skiing, bunco, chess — there is a very long list of meetup groups you can join. Just go to their website and do a bit of searching.

For example, I went to www.meetup.com/Womens-Hiking-Connection.

The description said:

> We are a group of mature, active women in our 40s, 50s, 60s, and up who enjoy getting out to hike and walk with nature. We may not be the first to reach the end of the trail, nor are we in a hurry to do so. Our interests are more along the lines of enjoying life, appreciating the beauty around us, and taking time to be in good company. We also cultivate a team approach, so everyone can list the hikes they want to do on the days they'd like to hike. Join a listed hike, or list your own and have other women join you. Hikes of all levels and abilities are offered. All women are welcome!

Don't see exactly what you love on Meetup? Can't find it in your town? Create a new meetup — you'll meet new people with your interest, and likely make a few friends more quickly.

People love golf. And Jim really loved golf. When he retired, he began working, not on a golf course, but in a small golf store. He describes his unique twist on this hobby: "I had once been a caddy as a college kid. I had also taught golf but not in years. Once I was retired, I went back and started giving golf lessons again. This took up fifteen to twenty hours a week. Hey, I am in seventh heaven. I meet a lot of students through the golf store, because they let me advertise there.

"I used the money I made to travel to major pro golf tournaments and watch the professionals play, especially the Women's PGA. I went to the Hawaiian Open and everywhere else they played. My ultimate thrill was the trip to Scotland I made with a group of other golf lovers to see the famous golf courses there. Now, that was something!" he says.

And you thought golf leagues were all you could do with golf! By exploring, you can find travel opportunities like Jim did. You can work at a golf course or at a pro shop and meet a lot of people and earn a paycheck too.

"The costs just spiraled out of control," explains Sally. She and her husband had bought a house that needed major remodeling. They spent over a year working on the project. Sally says, "Unexpected expenses were tapping a lot more money than we had budgeted. Finally we finished and moved into the house. That's when my darling husband issued a royal decree saying I could not hire an interior designer."

Sally loved interior design. This was the part of the project she had looked forward to. So with the budget blown, she got creative and put her thinking cap on. How could she decorate the house herself? She went to the mall and applied for a job at Pottery Barn.

"You get a 40%-off employee discount, so I was up for that," Sally says. "I could spend my paychecks buying things on sale and getting my discount on top of that. It made it all very affordable."

Right from the start, she was surprised by how much she enjoyed helping people with their home-decorating concerns. "I didn't expect to work at this job for very long. I was quite surprised that it was great fun to work and just talk about design ideas. It was like being in heaven," she said. "I've got no desire to quit anytime soon, even though the house is now completely decorated. I'm having too much fun. And the schedule is very flexible, making this an ideal situation," she says.

Retailers love hiring retirees. If you like a nice environment and want some extra income, plus that store discount, consider heading to the mall for a part-time job. They do hire seasonal help, so if you only want to work summers or for holidays, you can do that too.

Kathy's dogs were a big thing in her life. She had trained her own border collies, and when she got a new puppy she took it to an obedience class. The teacher was really impressed with her ability to work with the dogs and suggested she become a dog trainer. Kathy had been a lawyer living in a smaller community in Virginia. She was seventy-one when she decided it was time to stop practicing law and retire.

"The suggestion that I be a dog trainer just stuck in my head. I thought about the idea, realizing a lot goes into it. It's not just a simple thing you start doing," she says.

So she did an apprenticeship and took all the classes necessary to get the certification to become a lead trainer for dogs. "This is really my passion now," Kathy says. "But it's not for most people. Sure, it's a part-time kind of job, and I try to teach five classes a week when I'm not traveling. The money I earn is practically nothing. I enjoy it — that is why I'm there. A lot of time went into getting all those certificates to become a dog trainer. There is nothing more fun than working with dogs and trying to teach them to obey their owners so both pet and family can live in harmony. I love this job!"

Many new hobbies will require special training. Investigate, try it out, and if it feels right, then pursue it with a vengeance.

"I enjoy trying out new beers," says Bob, a soft-spoken but friendly retired special education teacher who enjoys going to local breweries and hanging out with friends. "I'm really interested in beer houses. Whenever I travel, I go to beer houses in all the new locales.

"I got a very exciting opportunity when my son decided to go to college for a year in China. I went over on several trips to visit him, and I explored many beer gardens. I met so many new people. I learned a lot but shared too. They were very interested in what beers are popular in the States."

Bob was able to sip many different beers from China and the neighboring countries. When he came back to the States, he told some friends about his experience. One mentioned it to the CEO of a small brewery in the area where Bob lived. That CEO contacted Bob and said, "We are very interested in promoting our beers in China. We found it to be a very hard and expensive experience. Let's talk about you maybe being a spokesperson for us. We'll send you over to select cities, where you could go to the breweries and just talk about our beers."

The company wanted to educate bartenders and have someone talk to the owners and, most important, to the patrons. Could Bob do that? He was learning the language, so, yes, he could. Now he spends a little bit of his retirement time getting paid as a beer spokesman. "Who'd have ever thought I'd be doing this? It's really just talking to people and being friendly. I found myself a perfect position when I wasn't even looking!" he says with a big smile.

Sometimes when you are immersed in your hobby, a job will find you like Bob's did. More often, you'll have to take the steps to land a job in that field. You may be surprised to learn that getting a part-time job is a lot easier than volunteering.

"I worry a lot about money, since I'm my sole support," explains Sonia. Before retiring, she'd been a customer service rep for a large phone company, and she didn't want to work long hours ever again. "I need to do something where I interact with people," Sonia says. "My pension is small and I need to add to it. Trouble is, everything pays minimum wage, and I want to make more money than that."

She took her problem to the temp agency, Manpower, to see if they could place her in a part-time job. Although she had great communication skills, she didn't really have any computer skills. "That proved to be a problem," Sonia explains. "Seems you need computer skills for just about everything available. Anything else was paying so low. So I sweetly asked the company representative, 'Don't you have something that pays more where you need good customer service skills?' I stressed how very friendly and outgoing I am. The rep came up with a job as an in-store food demonstrator. It's great. I get a four- to five-hour gig at the local grocery store or Costco and make between twenty-three and twenty-seven dollars an hour. I usually take on two or three days a week, and I love the job." Sonia makes up the food samples and hands them out to customers who walk by. "Easy-peasy" she says. "This job has great flexibility, and I make really good money for my time. It's ideal for me, and they love having boomers. I just show up and have no problems promoting the food product. Time just flies by."

More than three million people work for staffing or temporary agencies each week. These organizations seek out people for all kinds of jobs. They hire "contractors" —

aka you — to work on assignments. Definitely tell the agency worker where you'd like to work and doing what. They can likely place you in a hobby environment if you are specific when you describe the work and locale you wish to get a job in.

The Five Largest Staffing Firms in the United States
- **Allegis Group:** $8.63 billion
- **Adecco Group:** $4.627 billion
- **Randstad Holding:** $4.625 billion
- **Manpower Group Global** (NYSE: MAN): $3.54 billion
- **Robert Half International** (NYSE: RHI): $3.48 billion

You can accept a job, ask for another, or take certain days off. There is usually lots of flexibility. According to the American Staffing Association, the average wage is more than seventeen dollars an hour; some people in professional roles make more than a hundred dollars an hour. Search for staffing agencies in your area. The nice thing is that if you need some extra cash, you can sign up to work for a few weeks until you've made the cash you need.

Is Hollywood Calling?

Do you like movies? What about sci-fi? Ever thought about writing a screenplay?

Linda was sixty-six and had spent a great deal of time thinking about writing screenplays. A former lawyer, she had taken classes in screenwriting while she was still working. She had read books and even dabbled in trying to produce stories that might eventually get made into movies. When she retired, she began to write full-time.

"I was really serious once I retired," Linda explains. "I even moved to Los Angeles. I eventually sold options on three of my projects. Don't get too excited, though. You get a small sum simply for the right to hold the potential to maybe turn that screenplay into a film. Hollywood people call it 'being in development.' Me, I say it is really a black hole for the writer, as nothing happens for a long while. Either the option rights run out or move forward. I actually got lucky. One of my babies was made into a movie that was put into very limited release. It was a historical sci-fi story that, sadly, not many people ever saw."

Still, Linda lives in Los Angeles so she can be closer to the industry. She offers this advice: "It's very demoralizing if you're an older person in the movie business. Everyone is so insecure. It's just a tough business if you're not young. People have a tendency to think you're obsolete if you are old. Still, I'm doing it and it makes me very happy and creative. I plan to keep doing this as long as I can. Besides, the writing and character development really keeps my mind sharp. And I think that's very important as you age. I hold out the hope that I'll get a shot at having a movie made that people will flock to see." That seems to be every screenwriter's dream too.

Screenwriting, whether for TV or a movie studio, is not for the faint of heart. Rejection is the typical response. Before you slave away writing a script for your favorite sitcom, check to see if they accept unsolicited scripts. Most do not. They won't bother reading it. Your screenplay will just go in the trash.

There are various venues for an interest in movies. Theaters, of course, and TV networks, plus cable, with Lifetime and the Hallmark Channel, for example, buying and making a lot of movies. Online streaming services like Netflix and Amazon Prime have also gotten into the moviemaking business.

Mike wanted to go to film school and make movies, but when his girlfriend got pregnant, he married and went to business school, thinking it would lead to a more secure job. He worked as a manager in the Atlanta area and decided that Hollywood had just been a high school kid's dream.

"I still cling to a secret wish to be in movies and watch them be made up close," Mike told me. "Just before I retired, I read about a film being shot here, in Atlanta. I went online to find out who the producer was and to see if they needed extras. Seems they did. I applied and pretty much everyone who showed up got in. I was flying high. They dressed us up in period costumes, and we spent days on the set. I got to talk to other people involved in the production and, to my surprise, Atlanta is like the number one place that movies are made in the US. Lucky me!"

Mike found out that he could register with casting agencies if he wanted to be an extra. In the last few years, he's been in several films, plus a couple of TV commercials. "It's a blast. I'm living the dream — might be sixty-three but I'm living the moviemaking dream. And am I ever popular at parties now," Mike says. "Everyone wants the film lowdown. I spill the beans in small doses to keep people interested. I also invite my friends to go to the movie opening with me.

I have my own 'premiere.' Sometimes you can see me. Other times I'm part of the masses. But I'm always in there. It's the best hobby ever."

FOR LOVE OF THOSE DOGS

"I gave myself a retirement present," says Jeanette, who'd been a program specialist working in the corporate library of a Fortune 100 company when she retired at age sixty-three. "I bought myself an AKC purebred animal — a West Highland terrier, commonly called a Westie."

She discovered a local chapter for Westie owners and joined the club. Within a short time, a position as membership director opened up and Jeanette was asked if she would take it. She said yes. "I was interested in the dog club because I'm fascinated with show dogs. My new goal was to find out what kind of training was needed to show my dog, McDougal."

Dogs compete in these AKC purebred competitions to be "best of show" and get points necessary to win the title "champion." Jeanette had quickly found a new home — she enjoyed the sociability of the club and what the members were doing for the breed. And after a couple of years, they asked her to throw her name in the ring to be president. *Why not?* she thought. To her surprise, she became president. "I did a lot to support the breed and increase the club's events. A major highlight for me was watching the show dogs going into the ring, trying to become champions. It was captivating." Think of the Westminster Kennel Club Dog Show, only on a much smaller scale.

For nine years Jeannette served as the club president, writing newsletters, attending and planning events, educating people about the breed, and going to competitions.

At age seventy-five, she decided to step down to let someone else take over. Time for "new blood and new ideas," she says. "I have contributed everything I could. I'm not done, though, with my love of the show ring and this fabulous breed of dogs.

"You won't believe what I just did. For the first time ever, I bred my female Westie, Summertime. She's a sweet little girl and gave birth to six puppies. I sold each dog quickly and even had a waiting list."

These are expensive animals that can sell for two thousand dollars a dog (girls sell for even more). While some seniors might be seriously focused on the money, Jeanette says, "I was motivated because I wanted to have another dog or two I could show. I love these adorable Westies and the sport of showing them in the ring, competing against other dogs for a champion title."

MAKING THE MOST OF IT

When Lloyd retired, he and his wife decided to leave California and move to the Midwest to be near the grandchildren. That was enough for her, but he had a very difficult time in a new city where he knew no one. In California he'd had numerous friends and acquaintances. "I had a really important men's Bible group that I'd been part of for years. And honestly I discovered that making friends in your sixties proved to be quite a struggle for me."

One afternoon, Lloyd and his wife went to a community arts fair. He was struck by the beauty of a sculpture. He talked to the artist, who showed him pictures of the slab of stone he'd started with.

Lloyd said, "I left that arts fair and I could not get the idea of sculpting a stone out of my head. As soon as I got home, I went online and looked for an intro class. That's how the sculpting phase of my life started.

"It's me and the slab," he says. "I design and make things for the garden. As long as I can sculpt, I'm good. The creation process takes a long time. And it's just so rewarding to see the image shape up and finally, from a block of stone, you have this beautiful sculpture."

Lloyd is a resilient man and found a way to adapt to his new city and to do something new that fascinates him. This kind of hobby has a social side too. You might attend arts fairs to talk to other artists and get some new ideas. Lots of people are happy to share their creative secrets.

If you are interested in trying to advance your creative expression, go to a store that sells art supplies. Ask them about where you can take classes. Often a local artist teaches individuals or small groups. Also check out continuing education courses at your local community college. They often offer a wide range of art classes. In addition, search for "art classes" at Groupon.com. You'll find a few offerings and a discount on the first class too. I found "paint and sip" classes where you enjoy wine as you paint a scene. Groupon also had pottery, glassblowing, ceramics, drawing, and photography courses, as well as adult coloring.

ROOTING FOR THE HOME TEAM
"I've been addicted to watching sports on TV, whether it was football or college basketball. You could say I'm pretty obsessed with it," says Bernie.

When he retired, he missed having the guys at work to talk to about the games and sports news.

He went on Facebook and tried to reconnect with some people he knew in high school. Some still lived in the area, and with the pro football season coming up, he posted, "Hey, who wants to meet and watch the Giants season opener?" To his surprise, about seven people said yes, that they wanted to, so he made the arrangements to meet at a restaurant. He'd go early to get the table to be sure that they would have good seats in front of one of the big TV screens.

"I had an absolute blast!" Bernie says. "People in the sports bar get superexcited, screaming for the home team. We were cheering and yelling and laughing. It was so much more fun than watching it alone at home."

Everyone enjoyed the game, so Bernie suggested, "Hey, how about we do this every week until the Super Bowl?" Everyone said, "Yeah, that sounds great." A couple of people who happened to be in the bar said they'd come back every week and watch with them too. It proved to be such a great time that Bernie rounded up a group to watch a nearby college basketball team that is often quite good. "I spice things up with a football pool each week and a fun March Madness game. We all really get into the Final Four tournament.

"This has been a great hobby — a really fun thing to do," he continues. "Sometimes fifteen or twenty people — men and women — show up. Everybody's wearing shirts that advertise their support for their favorite team. Robin, lots of people should do this. It's so much fun, and you can make new friends to do other things with too. Every one of us has a big screen at home but it's not the same as watching with a lot of other people. Together you've got more spirit. You can yell anything and it is okay. We talk about the players, refs, and the games. I so enjoy it. My retirement has been great because I started this. I'm amazed that I organized it. I'm not someone who does that — but I took the risk and it really panned out."

Sometimes you have to be the one with the idea. You have to start something and involve others who share that hobby or interest. To get started, talk to a few of your friends and get a sense of what they would be interested in. Once you've decided on an activity, decide on the frequency of meetings, and block out your time. Get everyone's e-mail addresses. If you send out a reminder two days before the event, you'll have better attendance.

OLD INTERESTS
COME BACK TO LIFE

Give a bit of thought to activities you enjoyed in your childhood. As mentioned, some men rediscover motorcycle riding and it becomes a major focus in their retirement. For others, it could be a sport or any activity experienced a long while ago.

Peggy loved to read but had never joined a book club. When she retired she decided that maybe it was time to meet some new people, so she looked around for some clubs and found a local book club. She wrote to the organizer to find out the details, and it sounded interesting. She went to the first meeting, but the club specialized in a very specific genre that did not appeal to Peggy, so she graciously declined membership.

She was bummed out. And then the thought crossed her mind: *Why don't I start my own book club? I can make it be what I want it to be.* She e-mailed a few friends and asked if they had any interest. She told them that she wanted to read entertaining books and nothing too literary or depressing. To her surprise, five or six ladies said sure, they'd love to join. So she organized the first meeting and all the ladies came. And that's how she kicked off her book club. Peggy decided that whoever hosted the meeting was responsible for nominating three books. Everybody attending the meeting got to vote on which book they wanted to read. And the majority won. Doing it this way, people felt like they had a choice. Everybody liked the way Peggy had organized the book club. As the meetings went on, a couple of people invited a friend, so now the club has about ten members, and on average six or seven show up for a meeting. Peggy never misses it. Hosting goes from one lady to another, so it's not at the same person's house all the time. The host just puts out wine, soda, water, and some appetizers. It's pretty easy, and everyone seems to enjoy it. And, unlike some other book clubs, these ladies actually discuss the book, which was really important to Peggy. A couple of ladies who joined Peggy's group complained that the clubs they had tried before were way too social. People never talked about the books. Peggy's group has been going for two years and nobody's quit. To her mind, it's a big success, and she looks forward to going every month and reading books she probably never would've picked out herself.

Book clubs are very popular. Check the local library — libraries usually have many of these clubs. There might be one in your neighborhood, or through your church. Ask around to find out what's happening. And definitely consider starting your own club, like Peggy did.

DO YOU LOVE MUSIC?

Dave was a drummer when he was young. He and some guys had a band, much like every other music buff he knew. By college he'd left the drums at home, and once he started working as a software developer he never had time, so playing music became a thing of the past. Dave retired in his late fifties and decided to take some drum lessons and see if he could still do it. He found a local music shop and went to talk to them. "I wanted to see if I can still play. Do you rent drums?" he asked. Of course they did. So he loaded up the car and went home and put on some rock and roll and began to jam out. It was still fun. He then went back to the store and asked if they knew any bands with older guys who might need a drummer. They didn't but said he could put a notice on their board. The store sent a weekly e-mail to customers and always included people looking for gigs and those selling used stuff.

"Weeks went by and I forgot about it," Dave says. "Then one night my phone rang, and there was a group of men in their fifties, just like me. They played community events and their drummer had gotten hurt and couldn't play anymore. Did I want to audition? I was stoked! I also was smart enough to get a playlist, and I practiced their songs before I went. I sweated it out. But I fit in okay and so that is how I became part of the Rocking Oldies. We play at special events and summer festivals. We sure have a lot of fun. It's a great way to be a musician — my childhood secret dream finally came true!"

So many boomers love music. Many get involved with singing or playing an instrument. Music shops and talking to people in bands are the best ways to find opportunities to break into this field. Music shops often have a list of people who teach different instruments, so if you need instruction, start by asking at the music store.

SHOPPING!

Joanne loved to shop. It was one of her main hobbies when she was working. A customer service exec, she often traveled and found herself in malls. "I'd be walking through the mall or in a store, and I'd think about how the store could improve its service. It would be an automatic thought, as I went off to buy a new outfit or shoes."

In her midfifties Joanne retired but found that she got bored really quickly. She needed something interesting to do and found herself spending a lot of time in the malls. That's when the idea hit her. *I should be a mystery shopper.* She started networking with friends and made some calls to some of the big stores and restaurants in her area. They gave her the number of the agency they used. This is how she became a mystery shopper. "It's so easy. I go in and I shop. I eat or buy something and rate the experience. If I eat, they pay for my meal. When I buy something, I take it back that same day and write about the return experience too. The returns are often the most interesting — lots of people make you feel guilty about bringing something back. That's a no-no," she says.

You don't get much money for your time (about fifteen or twenty dollars an hour to do the shopping, plus another hour or so to write up the report). But that didn't matter to Joanne. She absolutely loved it. The job was a perfect fit with her customer service background and her love of shopping. She had to be careful to make sure she got the name of the person who waited on her, or people who didn't wait on her, or if too many sales people bugged her when she first walked into the store. Mystery shoppers are used by a lot of businesses that want to get feedback on what the customer experience is really like. Maybe this is a job you didn't know about but could enjoy. The nice thing about this position is that you can do it wherever you live, even if you are a snow-bird.

Dancing with Stars in Your Eyes

"I married my third wife when I was sixty, just as I was retiring," reveals Dave. "I adored Anne and had been single for over eight years when we met on Match.com. She told me that she enjoyed many things, and like most women she loved to dance. Me, I have two left feet and am embarrassed to go out on the dance floor. We planned on doing a luxury cruise for our honeymoon. Since she had been a dancer since high school and loved it so much, I went to Arthur Murray's and secretly signed up for dance lessons. I went for months. Crazy thing is, I enjoyed it. When we got married, was Anne surprised when I went out on the dance floor and was smooth and accomplished out there, shaking my booty. She thought it was the nicest present I could have given her."

The new couple returned home and got two free lessons from Arthur Murray as a wedding gift. Anne said, "Let's try ballroom dancing." So they did. It turned out to be how they spent the weekend. They would go to dances and eventually they joined in the competition. "It's all great fun for me," Dave explains. "She loves finding dresses and glamming it up for these things. I love the way she smiles at me when we dance. Been a crazy thing for us that I never thought I'd be doing. Not only do I do it, but I'm smiling like a fool the entire time, holding my adorable wife."

There are so many hobbies and interests you can pursue. Many have associations and national events you can get involved in. Sharing something with your spouse is a wonderful idea. The key factor is to remember that just because you haven't done something before or mastered it, doesn't mean you can't do it now. Be open to new experiences. Try new things. Say yes when people invite you.

SHARING THAT HOBBY

"Winter months are *cold* in Minnesota," says Deb, who loves quilting and would spend the cold weekdays working on her sewing machine to create beautiful quilts for her family and friends. Her daughter worked at a charity, and every year they asked Deb to create a beautiful quilt to raffle. She had a job working for a manufacturer as a procurement and planning coordinator. When her company offered an early retirement package at sixty-one, Deb took it.

One day she was at the quilting store talking with Pam, the owner, when Pam said she'd been thinking of offering some introductory quilting classes and wondered if Deb would be interested in teaching them. "I had never taught before," Deb says. "But I did teach my daughter to quilt, and she certainly loves the craft." So, "Let's try it," she told Pam.

"That is how my quilting classes began. Now I teach one or two times a week. I also get a discount on any supplies and fabric I buy. And of course I get paid for teaching. This is the perfect job — I'd do it for free but it's nice to earn a little extra cash too."

Marilee was a stressed-out manager when she retired at age sixty-three. She had a hobby collecting gems and minerals. Now that she wasn't working, she found she could pursue this hobby with gusto. Like most collectors, she's not alone. There are many people interested in "rocks," she says. She has made many new friends.

"I'm now a rock hound," Marilee explains. "My house is my display area. Shelves and cabinets show off different rocks I've picked up all over the place," she said.

She goes to numerous gem shows and belongs to a group that meets monthly. "The coolest thing ever was going to Tucson this year," Marilee says. "That city becomes a playground for the world of international gem and mineral trading, collecting, and bargain hunting when the Tucson Gem, Mineral & Fossil Showcase arrives. It's the largest show in the country and it is spread all over the city. In tents by the side of the road, in various hotels, convention centers, exhibit halls, etc. I went with a group of rock hounds and we had a fabulous time. I have to do this every year — it's the fantasy world for rock lovers like me."

Many people are collectors. Some collect baseball cards — especially rookie cards. Others collect coins, stamps, figurines, or porcelain. There are even wealthy men who collect cars. To each their own!

It's Showtime

Mark and Wendy lived in Florida during the winter. There was a woman in their community who loved producing big events. She had been the state director of a Miss America pageant and missed having all the camaraderie that comes with organizing big events. So she started *ShowTime,* a vaudeville-type show she put together for the local community. Wendy says, "It was absolutely amazing, the quality and all the laughs this production got. People came from miles and miles around to attend this spring event. I had done drama in high school and loved it, but my career as a school principal kept me super busy and never left time to do anything like this."

She and her husband joined the troupe. The first year she got in a skit with several other people. Overall, it was about a two-and-a-half-month commitment from the time you auditioned and said you wanted to be a part of the show to the actual performances. Wendy says, "It was so much fun and I made instant friends. The program had comedy and music, and we actually got standing ovations at the end of the performance."

For three years, it was the highlight of her Florida days. "It was absolutely the most fun thing I've done in the last two decades," she says. "Then the lady producer moved away. We'd all loved it so much that there was a big lobby wanting me to take it over. But I said no. That woman had worked for almost an entire year to come up with the ideas and do all the things necessary to make that production happen. I'd had a big, demanding job before I retired. Now I only wanted to have fun. No way was I taking on another job! But I really miss *ShowTime.* I wish we could find another group to do it. Everyone in our community still talks about it."

Understandably, you too may want to get involved in groups and fun projects but not create a full-time volunteer gig for yourself.

Being involved with theater is a popular activity. According to the American Association of Community Theatre, over forty-five thousand community-theater productions take place in the United States each year. They also offer classes in acting and programs on play production. Look around and you will likely find a local theater group you can get involved in. I heard from people who had done drama in high school or college and never again who as retirees took on acting roles or nonspeaking parts or worked on productions, directing, marketing, designing sets, and doing ticket sales and/or makeup. The one thing they have in common is that they love the experience of theater and have a lot of fun working in it. Retirement is meant to be enjoyed!

MAKING MONEY DOING YOUR HOBBY

Does the idea of making some money while working at a hobby appeal to you?

This is a new trend that's beginning to emerge among baby boomers in their post-retirement years. They get a fun, paying job. For many people, it's a comfort to be earning some income, whether it's a few hundred or a couple of thousand dollars. It may provide the psychological reassurance they need or just extra funds to help support a nicer retirement lifestyle.

Here are a few ways to monetize a hobby:

■ **Teach others to do what you love.** If you elect to be a tutor, you can make anywhere from twenty-five to fifty dollars an hour. Notifying local schoolteachers in the subjects you can tutor is the fastest way to get referrals. Advertising on a college campus by posting flyers with an e-mail or phone number tab is another. A third option is to join a tutoring organization like

Wyzant and work for them while they do the marketing.

Schools need tutors for all subjects. Think about what you can teach — painting, glassblowing, photography, music lessons. Offer cooking classes in your home or theirs. One lady offers a Groupon class where she comes to your home and teaches cooking to you and six to eight guests. From that she gets new students who want more cooking classes. Others teach languages; some teach computer skills. Offer your services on a local Facebook page. You can also teach through a community college or continuing education program. They are always on the lookout for teachers and new course offerings.

■ **Make it and sell it!** You do not need to have your own gallery full of pottery or paintings. You can create and then sell at local farmers' markets, community festivals, school or church craft fairs, etc. Whether it's baby clothes, sports-themed items, jewelry, cakes, glass vases — whatever you make, you can sell. If you need ideas, check out Etsy.com — a great place to advertise and sell handmade products.

■ **Selling memorabilia.** Are you a collector? Are baseball cards your thing? Maybe you go to spring training and get footballs signed by pro players. Signed NHL jerseys? Got an NBA card with a pro signature? Head online to eBay or go to a sports-card event and sell off some of your items. You can make some serious profit if you study the market and have popular memorabilia to sell. Bob goes to spring training for baseball. He hits Arizona one season and Florida the next, so he can cover all the teams. Most players are pretty laid back and willing to sign during training seasons. He collects signed baseballs and gets his wife to take a picture of the athlete signing it, to prove it's authentic. When his collection began to overrun the shelves at home, he decided to sell a few. He was shocked at how much money he could make doing this. It's a perfect hobby that is quite profitable, even after he subtracts his travel expenses.

■ **Teach the business of the hobby.** What do you know about? Can you teach others the skills they need to get new clients or sell more wares? If you know a great deal about managing the business of the hobby, you can teach others about it. One man retired and went on to teach how to run a photography business. He'd used photographers in his advertising and marketing career and did photography as a hobby. He put together a class and offers it through a continuing education department, teaching the business skills to be more successful making money as a photographer. Major hit — all his classes fill to capacity. He now goes to photography conferences and events and teaches there. By teaching new entrepreneurs and struggling business owners, you can make a big difference and some nice cash.

■ **Speak or write about your hobby.** Jordan loves the stock market and studies it daily. Over the years he's been very successful at investing. His neighbors wanted him to put on a class about handling investments, and he volunteered to teach it. Only ladies showed up. They devoured his information and wanted another, more in-depth class. He developed the class but this time he charged twenty-nine dollars, and still his class filled up — but only with ladies. He realized he was sitting on a tiny gold mine. He began a series of investing courses in the area just for women.

■ **Writing, editing, and proofing can be a profitable hobby.** Many people like the idea of writing, but did you realize you could write about your hobby and earn some money? Best option is look for companies that need writers for their newsletters or website content. Also, get advertisers for your blog or hobby website. You can make money every month as long as they get what they want — eyeballs reading your work.

■ **Offer a service.** Like cooking? Offer your assistance to help neighbors out with a hot dinner for a small fee. Love pets? You can become a dog walker or be a pet sitter. One lady loved to paint murals, so she put some pictures of what she'd done on the neighborhood Facebook site and got several calls from eager people wanting to hire her to create murals for them in their homes and businesses.

TIME TO FINALIZE A PLAN ABOUT YOUR HOBBIES

For Those Seeking a Paid Position
In part 1 you identified several hobbies you would like to be involved with. Some lead more easily to paying jobs. Identify the single hobby you want to focus on.

What hobby would you be most interested in turning into a new job?

_____

Brainstorm the types of paid positions that involve that hobby.

_____

_____

Searching online and talking to reference librarians at your local library can help you identify jobs where you could work in that hobby area.

Websites or places to look for these jobs include:

_____

_____

_____

Who should I network with to obtain a paying hobby job I might enjoy?

_____

_____

_____

What are the action steps I need to take to find this job?

_____

_____

_____

_____

For Those Just Looking to Explore a Hobby
  for Fun
What hobby would you be most interested in pursuing?

_____

_____

_____

_____

Narrow down your options so you can start focusing on one area first. Searching online, investigating if there are meet-ups in your area, and talking to business owners related to the hobby can help you identify groups and activities to get involved with.

Who should you network with?

_____

_____

_____

_____

What steps do you need to take to make this hobby part of your life?

Hobbies can change by season and by location. You may pursue very different things in winter and summer. Engaging in new activities makes life interesting and will enable you to meet new people. Most important, only stick with the hobby if you are having fun. If that changes or the group doesn't click with you — keep on looking.

RESOURCES

Always check my website, where we keep up-to-date listings of websites and terrific resources. Things can change quickly! Go to www.MyRetirementReinvention.com/resources.

CHAPTER 10
TRAVEL

Oh the places you can go!

There is nothing better to stimulate our minds and hearts than travel. What is your fantasy? Spending the winter on a sun-drenched, sandy beach? Living in Europe for a month? Going on a world cruise? I personally want to do the last one but only after I make it to Australia and go snorkeling in the Great Barrier Reef.

We all have dreams about travel. Some retirees travel strictly for leisure, while others combine work and travel to help mitigate the cost of the experience. Once you are no longer working, you have the time to make your dreams come true.

WHAT OTHERS ARE DOING
Forbes reviewed travel studies and determined retirees' favored kinds of travel. Although many enjoy a variety of vacation

spots, familiar locations remain the most popular. Where we stay once we get there, though, is quickly changing. Globally, almost one million Airbnb users are over sixty and seeking out a home to enjoy their vacation or travel experience like a local would. In fact, some people stay home and rent out a room via Airbnb once the kids have moved out. They enjoy meeting and conversing with guests, plus they earn some extra money too.

Adventure travel is up, and so are retirees taking RV trips. Biking is replacing golf as a popular option for active holidays. Learning is becoming extremely popular. Educational tours and programs that combine travel and learning are booming. And of course there is cruising. Around-the-world cruises grew to more than twenty-three million passengers, 52% of whom are age fifty or older. Solo travel as well as multigenerational travel are on the upswing.

Where do boomers like to go? *Forbes* says retirees (age fifty-plus) preferred these travel destinations.

In the United States
- Hawaii
- New York
- California

- Alaska
- Florida

In the World
- Italy
- Australia
- England
- Ireland
- France

Chris wrote to me to say that he was making plans to sail around the world. "I bought my first sailboat with lawn-mowing money when I was eleven. I dragged it two blocks, across the neighbors' front lawns, to a nearby canal, plunked it in the water, and explored my little bit of Tampa Bay. It was the first of five boats, slowly graduating up to our current boat — a forty-one-foot, around-the-world cruising sailboat. Mostly, I've spent days and weekends trying to create the perfect sail shape and chatting with whomever I could convince to come along."

He wrote that his lovely wife, Michelle, looked at him one day and said wistfully, "You know I love you like crazy, but I really miss the world, and Minnesota is so far from everything." Her message to him was clear: "If I'm to be happy, I need to get back to traveling the world." That resonated with

Chris and a new plan went into full motion.

Next summer Chris and Michelle will hug the kids good-bye and sail off on their adventure. They will sail through the Great Lakes to Newfoundland and across the North Atlantic to England. They plan to explore the British Isles, the western coast of Europe, and the Mediterranean until they're ready to return to the Caribbean, through the Panama Canal, and out into the Pacific. Quite a plan! It may not be your utopia but for many sailors out there, it is theirs.

Many people would love to explore the world but need to find a job to make it happen. Chris and Michelle plan to teach English at international schools to finance some of their dream. There are lots of opportunities to make travel the center of your Retirement Reinvention, as this chapter will detail.

Travelers' number one wish is to experience the northern lights in person.

EXPERIENTIAL TRIPS
TV travel host and author Rick Steves specializes in trips to Europe. His website advocates smart, affordable, perspective-broadening travel. He encourages Ameri-

cans to travel as "temporary locals." He helps travelers connect much more intimately and authentically with Europe — and Europeans — for a fraction of what mainstream tourists pay. A popular TV guest on PBS, Rick Steves's organization offers dozens of tours each year. These trips vary in length from seven to twenty-one days, and they retail for two thousand to five thousand dollars plus airfare. They do have wonderful testimonials, and many people seem to find them to be a terrific experience. Learn more at www.ricksteves .com.

Instructional trips appeal to many retirees. Colleges offer some such programs. Road Scholar offers experiences that attract highly educated and interesting attendees. Several retirees mentioned that they had participated in various outdoor adventure experiences. All of these were short-lived but very memorable.

Bicycling was Lois's favorite pastime. When she retired, at sixty-two, from her job as an elementary school teacher, she had more time to put into this hobby. At sixty-eight, she went off on a European tour with Road Scholar (www.roadscholar.org, formerly known as Elderhostel). Lois went on the bike trip with her forty-five-year-old daughter. Only one participant needed to be over fifty-five, which is a little-recognized fact. Mom and daughter agreed on a bicycle tour of the Provence region of France. For fourteen days they bicycled from town to town and stayed in nice inns. A van followed in case they had any technical issues with their bikes.

"We had fourteen people in the group," Lois explains, "all from the US. Generally, breakfast and dinner were provided. It was delicious — fine local cuisine. The best part was that at each destination, or at sites along the way, we were met by knowledgeable guides who took the group around and gave us a true picture of this French area. It was fascinating. Our tour leader was from Belgium, spoke fluent English, and was professional and helpful. It was a nice mix of tour time and free time. I was hooked. What a unique way to see Europe and really experience the countryside and learn the history of the region."

Lois has taken five bike trips in total. Two other trips to Europe were with International Bicycle Tours, including barge/bike trips — one when she was seventy-five and one last spring, when she was seventy-eight. "My friends were no longer strong enough to do an extended bike trip, so I went alone.

The group tour went through Belgium. I'm so glad I didn't miss this. I never felt 'alone' for even one minute. The tour was a seniors-only trip, and the people were so funny and full of life. The trip was a terrific experience," she says.

In comparing the two organizations, Lois noted that both do a good job setting up the tours, getting you from place to place, etc. Where Road Scholar excelled was in its guides for local attractions. They were very knowledgeable and ready when you arrived. That said, Road Scholar trips are more expensive but have been around since 1975. While you are not staying in hostels, you are not doing five-star hotels either but safe, comfortable, local accommodations chosen to give you a feel for the local culture. They have trips that accommodate almost all activity levels, with a variety of different activities such as bicycling, rafting, hiking, walking, woodworking, opera, archaeology, and history. There are even intergenerational trips designed for seniors and their grandchildren.

Are you the curious type? Interested in unique programs that build your knowledge of another part of the world? The Smithsonian Institution offers travel programs (www.smithsonianjourneys.org) that further its important mission — the "increase and diffusion of knowledge." Its tours and cruises enrich travelers' lives. A proven leader in culturally enriching, expert-led travel, Smithsonian Journeys offers more than 350 trips lasting up to thirty days, on all seven continents. Every program includes unforgettable experiences that uncover the authentic culture of each destination and provide access unavailable to most travelers. The tour experts are world-class leaders in their fields.

LIVING LIKE A KING AND QUEEN

This couple definitely did it their way. Michael wrote me this long story about how he lived out his unique fantasy. He wanted to partake in the lifestyle of the rich and famous. This is how he lived out his dream.

I'm not sure exactly how we arrived at the idea of being caretakers, but once we started reading the ads for domestic couple positions, working for the ultra-wealthy, the hook was set. When we saw the kind of money that we could make, the kinds of places we could live, and the fringe benefits, we knew we wanted in.

I was always kind of a gearhead — liked mechanical things and loved being outdoors — but I ended up with an inside sales, cubicle-world job that I absolutely hated. When I lost that job, it turned out to be the best thing that could have happened, because it forced me to do some hard thinking about how I wanted to spend the rest of my life.

My wife, Mary, ran a successful day-care business. She loved working with kids and it was a good business.

We were both in our late fifties and ready to reinvent ourselves. At the time, I kept seeing all these executives getting multimillion-dollar "golden parachutes." In fact, I can remember joking that since we didn't get a golden parachute ourselves, maybe we could latch onto the ankles of someone who did. And, in fact, that's almost exactly what we ended up doing.

Once we decided what we wanted to do, the question was how. We sent out a bunch of applications but weren't getting much in the way of responses. The upper-echelon domestic couple jobs are generally handled by employment agencies, and they flat out won't talk to you unless you have a minimum of two years' experience working in a wealthy household. We had the right skills and were well suited for the job, but we couldn't get past the "gatekeepers." I'm pretty good at selling myself, but we needed to be able to deal directly with an employer.

In January an ad appeared in the *Caretaker Gazette* for a domestic couple position in Aspen, Colorado, that seemed perfect for us. And it wasn't through an agency. We sent an application right out but got a nice note back saying that the position had been filled. About three months later, the Aspen job turned up in the *Gazette* again. We put in another application, and one day the phone rang — it was them! After some back-and-forth, we were offered the job.

It was an entry-level job in both pay and duties, but the important thing was we were in. Surprisingly, my wife's day-care experience was key — they had nine dogs and figured if Mary could take care of kids, she could take care of dogs. The second helpful fact was that we'd lived at high altitude before. Their house is at nine thousand feet. The couple they'd hired couldn't cope with the altitude and had left after three months.

So we packed up our car and left our home in Grand Haven, Michigan, for Aspen. The job included a free apartment — it was over the garage but very nice and had the same view they did. We liked to joke that it was a million-dollar-apartment view.

The house in Aspen was eight thousand square feet and quite a showplace. It's been featured in numerous magazines, as well as the *Wall Street Journal.* It was valued at fifteen million dollars at the time and was full of art, antiques, furs, jewelry, and who knows what else. When they weren't there, we were responsible for everything, plus their beloved dogs. It was intimidating, working in a house like that. I never touched anything I didn't have to — some little knickknack on an end table might well cost more than our car.

It turned out to be a much more difficult and complicated job than we could have ever imagined. The level of complexity in a house like that boggles the mind. Aside from the sheer physical labor of caring for it, inside and out, you have to understand how it all works and know (or learn) about an incredible number of subjects.

I also had to schedule, supervise, and deal with the small army of outside contractors (when I couldn't fix it myself) it takes to keep a place like this running smoothly. But by far the hardest part of the job was dealing with the personalities of the owners. Multimillionaire types and their spouses have big egos and big personalities, to put it charitably. They aren't patient people either; they are used to having everything they want *now*. At times I wanted to tell them that carpenters and plumbers didn't generally have the same kind of response time as, say, the fire department, but of course I didn't. I just put together a team of contractors who understood our "special needs" (at a price) and would get there quickly.

But there were many perks to the job too. We'd start our day by loading up a couple of dogs and taking them someplace nice to hike. Mary and I love walking and hiking. We couldn't believe we were getting paid to go hiking in such a beautiful place!

We spent two years in Aspen and learned a lot. But we wanted to be near our family in Michigan and started looking for jobs that were closer to home. We took a job in Auburn Hills, Michigan. This was a whole different world. The house was thirteen thousand square feet plus a guest house and a three-story boathouse with ballroom. There were ten acres of mowed lawn, with intricate landscaping, four fountains, a pond, a beach, and ten acres of woods, all to be maintained by me.

The job was a real learning experience, and we added a lot of new skills to our résumés. Mary cooked, and we served at parties. I was bartender. We helped put on larger events with more than one hundred fifty guests. And I played chauffeur in the Bentley. They liked how we ran things, and after a few months the job went from caretaker couple to a true estate-manager couple position. They asked us to also manage their oceanfront estate in Florida. Mary and I began spending more of our time managing people who did the work, and I learned quite a bit about running an estate long distance (with occasional visits).

After two years, our current job essentially fell into our laps. The house is twenty-two thousand square feet, plus a pool house, carriage house, and three-thousand-square-foot wine cellar. There are twenty acres of mowed lawn, but there's a full-time groundskeeper, so I have some help. Plus we got a big raise in pay along with top-notch health insurance. The owners have turned out to be the sweetest people we've ever worked for, and they treat us great. One September they sent us to their vineyard in Napa for a week to dog-sit. They paid for the whole trip, had us stay in the guesthouse, gave us lots of free wine, a new Jeep to use, and told us to go have fun when we weren't watching the dogs.

I suppose the moral of our story is that I now have a new career that quite honestly has turned out to be the best, most challenging, and most satisfying job I've ever had. Mary didn't realize how burned-out she'd gotten until she got away from the day-care business, and in spite of working very hard is finding her new role a very welcome change.

The domestic couple business sure isn't for everyone — while the job descriptions make it sound pretty easy, the reality is anything but. At times we can't believe we actually get paid for some of the things we do, but the majority of the time it's the hardest job either of us have ever had. There are a lot of potential pitfalls. It's an odd combination of menial tasks and huge responsibility. I might clean up dog dirt one minute then hop in a Maserati, Bentley, or classic Cobra 427 to get gas or take it in for service. While driving cars like that might sound like fun, it is until you realize that a flawless Cobra is worth a million bucks, and if you scratch it, you'd be out of a job. It's always a bit of a "high-wire act." It's fast paced, high pressure, intense, and you're on duty 24-7 when the owners are in residence.

Now, that is a different lifestyle. For potential house sitters and caretakers, there are jobs that suit anyone's interests and abilities. There are jobs in big cities, rural places, full-time career-type jobs, part-time laid-back-type jobs, ranch or farm jobs — you name it. And you can work in exotic locales all over the world. Mike said to me, "It's a wonderful lifestyle, and our only regret is that we didn't get into it sooner."

This may not be the kind of work or travel experience you've considered. Maybe you didn't even know these kinds of opportunities for house-sitting and caretaking existed. I spoke to Gary Dunn, the editor of the *Caretaker Gazette* (www.caretaker.org), where people advertise caretaking and house-sitting jobs. He offered some ideas of actual work opportunities from around the world from a recent newsletter:

AUSTRALIA — Looking for a mature couple in New South Wales who are cat lovers, and who would like to care for our affectionate house cat from approximately

December 23 to January 10, and then from mid-June to the end of summer.

RANCH HELP needed in Prescott, Arizona. Need some part-time work in exchange for a two-bedroom, two-bath 1,500 sq. ft. home in an upscale location.

BELIZE — Wanted, a semiretired couple to caretake for no less than four weeks anytime from March to November. Your primary responsibility is having a presence on the property. Duties include care and feeding of six dogs, fishes, watering young plants.

NATIONAL PARK HOST from May 21 through September 1, 2016. Must have your own RV.

LIVE-IN CARETAKER needed in Port St. Lucie, Florida, for my independent delightful grandmother. You will need to cook, grocery shop, and take her to church and her doctor appointments.

This is a travel-work opportunity you might want to consider. Now you know these options are out there, and a little more about the work and job skills needed to land them.

TEACHING ENGLISH ABROAD

The desire to live and work abroad is among the fastest growing for boomers shaping their Retirement Reinvention. Most are doing this by teaching English. Long popular with college students, organizations such as WorldTeach, Peace Corps, and International Volunteer HQ now welcome baby boomers. Over half a million American retirees receive Social Security benefits in countries other than the United States, according to the Social Security Administration. (That figure does not count those baby boomer expatriates who aren't yet eligible for Social Security or have postponed taking it.) While most choose to go to Europe, Central American countries are becoming more popular, with some boomers heading to Asia too.

Are you a retiree looking to teach abroad? Teaching in exchange for room, board, and a small salary can be a very interesting way to kick off your Retirement Reinvention. Whether you seek a little adventure in Europe, want to make a difference in a small village in Africa, or wish to live on a tropical beach in Latin America, teaching English offers an endless array of great international opportunities.

Hundreds of thousands of English speakers from all walks of life are hired to teach English abroad each year, and in the vast majority of cases prior teaching experience, or even a college degree, is not required. Some teachers work on full-time contracts. Others tutor, and many elect part-time positions.

The demand for English teachers worldwide is high. However, it is worth noting that some countries offer more opportunities and more accommodating job markets than others, especially to more mature travelers, when it comes to age restrictions for teaching English abroad.

Briefly, here are some regions and countries that make great options for older travelers who want to live and teach English outside the United States.

Latin America is a gold mine for English-teaching opportunities. Latin America offers a wide range of choices when it comes to destinations and teaching opportunities. In addition, the cost of living — including rent, food, and medical care — in most Latin American nations is low, and the vast majority of schools are happy to hire more mature teachers.

Costa Rica is a tropical paradise where the cost of living is low and the people are known for an easygoing approach to life known as *pura vida* (pure life). Boasting some of the most beautiful rain forests and beaches in the world, Costa Rica is hard to beat when it comes to quality of life, outdoor recreation, living costs, and high demand for native English-speaking language instructors.

Mexico offers a vast array of fascinating cultural experiences and spectacular natural beauty. It is also one of the largest job markets in the world for teaching English abroad, and age discrimination is not a factor.

Southeast Asia offers hundreds of thousands of opportunities to teach the five hundred million people who are learning English.

China is the largest job market in the world, but opportunities are limited mostly to retirees under the age of sixty.

Cambodia, known for the ancient ruins of Angkor Wat, idyllic beaches, and faded colonial charm, isn't as large or as prosperous as nations like South Korea or Japan, but the demand for English teachers is booming, and, unlike in many other Asian countries, age is not a restricting factor, and those without a degree can gain employment as well.

Thailand offers something for everybody, from turquoise waters and white sandy beaches to colorful street life in Bangkok and lush highlands in the north. English-teaching jobs are concentrated in major cities like Bangkok and Chiang Mai, but schools, language institutes, and even universities employ English teachers throughout the country.

Western Europe in general has stringent visa requirements, so EU countries like France, Spain, and Italy are more challenging places to find work opportunities.

Eastern Europe is another story. Nations like Poland, Hungary, Croatia, and Bulgaria have a huge demand for English teachers and native English speakers will have no difficulties procuring a work visa.

The Czech Republic, located in the heart of Europe, has developed into an important location for business, investment, and tourism in recent years, increasing the demand for English teachers. Your best bet is looking in the capital city of Prague, where you will find work opportunities in public and private venues, and as a private tutor. Schools are willing to help with living arrangements as well.

Russia, situated as far east in Europe as you can travel, offers an opportunity to live in a mysterious and fascinating country and interact with its people. Most schools require some sort of TEFL certification (see below) but will help out with your work visa once hired.

The Middle East is particularly good for those with teaching experience and credentials. The Arab nations of the Persian Gulf offer relatively lucrative teaching opportunities that typically include benefits like free airfare, free housing, and health insurance. Many teaching opportunities can also be obtained locally in countries like Egypt and Morocco.

Saudi Arabia has a growing need for teachers, due to a government initiative to introduce the English language to university students who in turn look at the international job market. Riyadh (the capital) and Jeddah are the largest cities and are both known to be very safe. No TEFL certificate is required, but it is recommended, and teaching experience is highly sought after.

United Arab Emirates (UAE) is one of the most rapidly progressing countries in the Middle East and the perfect location for teachers looking for a rewarding experience. Teaching English here will immerse you in a blend of traditional Arabic culture and the ultramodernity of Dubai, with its futuristic feel. Most jobs require teaching experience and a commitment of two years, so make sure you qualify and are up to the terms.

If you want to consider teaching abroad, do a bit of self-analysis:

- Are you okay doing this alone?
- Do you handle unfamiliar or uncomfortable situations well?
- Do you have patience?
- Can you teach others?
- Will you be able to live a very streamlined life in a dormitory-like setting

and do without many of the comforts of home?

- Financially are you okay with just breaking even, or do you need to be able to save money?
- Do you have money you can use to supplement your income for additional travel? (Hint: Southeast Asia, China, and South Korea pay very well.)

Although no teachers' certificate is required, I recommend you acquire TEFL certification. "TEFL" stands for "teaching English as a foreign language," and certification is available by going to TEFL.org.

You don't need a degree in education, prior teaching experience, or even a college degree to get paid to teach English abroad. Find more info at www.MyRetirement Reinvention.com/resources.

Choose carefully where you'd like to teach. Issues vary by hiring company and by country. Some countries have age restrictions as they have mandatory retirement ages that will exclude many over age sixty. Other places have no restrictions.

Do your own research. A good place to start is the website Go Overseas (www .gooverseas.com). It lists more than nine hundred programs you can explore. This website also offers some sage advice about different areas of the world you could teach in.

If you aren't sure which countries to look at first, Asia is probably the best region for newbie teachers. You can find a decent-paying job with no teaching experience and the cost of living is relatively low in many places.

HOW TO APPLY

If you want to teach abroad, you need a résumé that is a bit different from the one you used to hunt for a job in the States. Outline your coaching, tutoring, or teaching experience (paid or unpaid) along with travel experience that may make you more adaptable to this type of work. If you have strong writing ability demonstrated by published work — a blog, articles, website content, books — these need to be mentioned. Past skills that show you are adaptable and flexible should also be emphasized. Past work experience and any languages you speak (beyond English) should be stated clearly too. If you have a college degree, and/or TEFL certificate, make sure you highlight that as well.

Expect contact via e-mail and for the company to do a Skype interview (videoconferencing over the Internet) before you get accepted. Companies may be anywhere in the world. Skype is a great way for them to determine if you are capable of the job, smart, but also "have a personality," and can interact with customers, partners, managers, and other executives. It helps them get a "feel" for a candidate and a better understanding of their personality.

Video interviews via Skype can present a new challenge to the job hunter. Candidates need to be comfortable using Skype and able to recover if there is a tech glitch in transmission. Appearing to be technically savvy is vital to making a good impression. Practice using Skype before the interview and expect several questions that ask you to outline your past work experience, offering examples of how you performed and behaved on the jobs.

SKYPE INTERVIEW DOS AND DON'TS

Learning to use Skype is handy if you're moving to a different part of the States or to a new country. It's great for keeping in touch with friends and family. And Skype is often used for interviewing people in other locations too. Here are some key things to know if you are about to have a Skype interview.

Ask in advance for all the details about the interview. What position is it for? How long will the interview be? How many people are interviewing you? Who will they be? Don't expect the interviewer to volunteer much, so ask and call back a second time if you need more clarification.

Don't start out by apologizing for your being unfamiliar with Skype. That is not what the employer wants to hear. Practice using this technology several times, so you know how to connect, reconnect, adjust the volume, etc.

Pay attention to what you are wearing: dress as you would if you were appearing in person. Select a conservative suit and be sure you do not have any plaids or bright prints, as these don't look good when viewed via a monitor.

Test the equipment. Make sure the background is uncluttered and professional (not the kitchen). Be sure the room is completely quiet and that you will have no interruptions during the interview.

Check the lighting on your face. Sometimes you don't realize how awful the picture looks, with shadows aging you. Be sure you have excellent light (use an extra lamp or sit by the window) to be sure you come across as professional and interested, with energy and enthusiasm.

Practice! Get used to the camera and talking to your computer. Try not to move around or fidget. Nervousness and movements are magnified on video. You must seem confident, comfortable, and enthusiastic about the job. Smile often — you will come across as a warmer, more likable person.

Relax and rely on your preparation, and keep your answers under sixty seconds — with videoconferencing shorter answers are better. If possible, try to make it a conversation. Ask questions as you go along.

For more job-interview help, read my book *60 Seconds and You're Hired!,* available in bookstores and online from Amazon .com.

LIVING A DREAM

"At age sixty-four, I am healthy and still enjoy exploring new locales and living in another country," says Linda, whose goal was to improve her Italian by living in Italy. She needed a rent-free, easy caretaker-type role and found something that proved to be ideal. "I've always loved to travel, ever since I took my first trip to Europe, back in the 1970s, on a Eurail pass, with girlfriends. I have lived in Mexico for five years, and

France for two, as an ESL (English as a second language) teacher," she says.

"A lead in the *Caretaker Gazette* caught my eye," Linda continues. "I could live rent-free in Tuscany. I immediately e-mailed and told them about my background and interest, and that I speak basic Italian and wanted to improve it by living in the country and studying it at the same time. I got a positive reply and that is how I spent May, June, and July of this past year in Italy.

"I was surprised to learn that the owners of the villa I worked at were a count and countess. Their property, the Villa di Corliano, was a fifteenth-century villa, and is now a bed-and-breakfast, as most wealthy or royal Italians can no longer pay the high taxes and must earn income from their properties. My position required that I stay in the villa every night, beginning at midnight, and do two hours of light gardening and cleanup in exchange for the rent. I stayed in the official guardian's room at the top of a spiral staircase and was there in case of emergencies, or if a guest forgot the door code or needed a cab or something."

The villa and grounds are of exceptional beauty — full of trees, animals, and history. The gardening aspect of Linda's job was to tidy and clean the grounds immediately surrounding the villa, trim the roses, rake a few leaves, etc., as three other full-time gardeners looked after the grounds.

"On a typical day," Linda explains, "I would be up early, have a light breakfast in my room, then walk down to the gardens. The mornings were always spectacularly beautiful, with the birds and magnificent trees (my favorite was one planted by Napoléon's army). I would trim the bushes, and clean up, and enjoy the fresh air and peacefulness of the surroundings. Midmorning, I might buy an espresso at the bar or if it was a market day, catch the bus in front of the villa and go into Pisa, about ten minutes away, have coffee in the market, and shop and enjoy the activities. I would also go to nearby Lucca, a charming walled medieval town. I studied Italian daily and practiced with the staff and anyone I met, and got better and better as time went by. Needless to say, the food and wine were delicious and the people very hospitable.

"This experience was like living in a fairy tale. The count and his wife took me to the beach, to parties, and showed me the countryside. It was a lovely experience. I enjoy meeting people, and I'm very flexible and curious — key traits for people seeking work and travel experiences."

IMMERSION PROGRAMS

"We take a lot of baby boomers on our service trips," says Chris Mackay, cofounder of Crooked Trails (www.crookedtrails.org), a company that offers immersive travel and purpose-filled opportunities in Asia, South America, Central America, and Africa. The volunteers experience the culture by working and living side by side with people in the community, sharing meals and often even staying in their homes. "We want to have people connect culturally in a rich way. You can select a trip by the community we serve or by the cause closest to your heart, such as building a school or a healthy kitchen for a family. The people you meet in these tiny outlying villages are thrilled to meet you. And if you are an elder, you are revered," says Chris. "But it is complete immersion — no one in these villages speaks any English at all. Still, joy, caring, and appreciation are universal in smiles, hugs, nods, and gratefulness that you are there. On one trip we took Josie, a seventy-eight-year-old lady who proclaimed this was not a vacation, it was an experience! She then wanted to do another trip, this time to Nepal. I explained that Nepal was a rigorous trip and lacked every creature comfort. I pointed out there were only outdoor squatting toilets, one slept on the ground, etc. Not only did Josie go, but she brought two friends — one seventy-nine, the other eighty. And they did amazingly well." The ladies worked on building a school in Nepal alongside the local villagers, learning to communicate without words as indeed none of the villagers spoke English. Josie said it was a rare opportunity to become immersed in different cultures while helping some of the world's poorest people. "It was so meaningful and profound," she told Chris about her experience.

These trips run about twenty-five hundred dollars plus airfare, for ten days, and each is customized. Recently, for example, Chris arranged for Juan, age fifty-nine, his wife, and another couple to visit Cuba. Juan's grandfather had played the trombone in Cuba decades before, and he wanted to see and experience his grandpa's homeland. Juan brought along Grandpa's trombone, as he is a musician too. The highlight of his trip was playing the trombone with musicians from a local village. "It was a life-changing experience," he told Chris.

Translators do go along on these trips, but much is learned without words. Travelers realize that as much as they give, the people they meet make them feel like honored guests and that they are getting even more back. When asking about trips, people often get queasy about hygiene issues: the lack of toilets and privacy you get in these rural villages. Chris says that when the travelers actually get there, all these worries fall by the wayside when they meet the people who are so happy and honored that they are there.

Other options abound. If you are looking for a trip with a purpose, check out those sponsored by church groups, charities, and immersion programs like the ones we've just seen.

LIVING AND WORKING ABROAD

Some people simply want to live in another culture, and whether that means heading to Mexico, Costa Rica, the Caribbean, Australia, Asia, or South America, there are ways to make this affordable.

Terry had spent decades working as a carpenter and house contractor. After falling off a ladder, he could no longer do the work. He had vacationed in Panama every year for over a decade and decided he wanted to live there as part of his Retirement Reinvention. It was the only place he felt he could afford an ocean view, and he bought a small house within walking distance to the beach. If you think living as an expatriate is appealing, look hard under the hood before you sell off your US possessions and head to some foreign land. Terry commented that this country of just four million people has a very low cost of living, but no place is perfect. Each has its own problems too. Terry pointed out that in Panama the cost to build, purchase, or rent a house or condo will be substantially less than in the States. Property taxes are extremely low and many times don't exist at all, due to government incentives. The cost of utilities is very low too. Water, for example, runs about fifteen dollars a month, though electricity is equal to, or more than, in the States. "You definitely enjoy a higher standard of living in Panama," he says. "They have real decent health care too. The weather is perfect for me — at sea level it's 85–90°F. Panama is a small and narrow country, with a pretty well-sized mountain range running down the middle. Head up into the mountains and temperatures drop. It will be about 75°F in the Boquete area. Serious crime is low, and that's another nice thing. Of course, you can't leave your phone in the car for a minute or it'll likely be gone. And forget about customer service — it takes a lot longer to get any repair work done here. I tried finding odd jobs the first year but found that laborers and construction people were not paid very well at all. Instead, I found a part-time job driving a tour bus. I'm a friendly guy and really enjoy this position."

According to The Street (www.thestreet .com), which has a website for Americans thinking of retiring to places like Panama, Panama is not "just like the US, only cheaper." It has its own culture and way of doing things. It's on "island time," meaning people are not as prompt and things don't get done as quickly or as efficiently. Panama has fabulous diversity in many ways. It has jungles, cosmopolitan areas, colonial cities, and modern skyscrapers, all easily accessible and close to each other. You can swim in the Pacific and the Caribbean on the same day, and at some places in the mountains you can see both bodies of water from the same spot. Want to go shopping at high-end malls and eat at fancy restaurants? Panama has them. Want to buy handmade jewelry from Kuna Indians or "go native" in a sparsely inhabited area? No problem. Care to be around North American expats? There are places where you can speak English to pretty much everyone you see and go to happy hours with your North American friends every day. Don't want to be around expats at all? Panama can accommodate you too. Want to be part of a close-knit community that can provide support and also greater meaning through helping others? The expats in Panama are brilliant at that. On the downside, the country pours its sewers into the ocean and many beaches are not safe for swimming.

International Living magazine and others annually publish lists of "best" countries to retire to.

Interestingly, *US News & World Report* says you can reinvent your life and live better in these top ten places:

1. **Carvoeiro, Algarve, Portugal.** This is a best-kept secret, and for the last three years *Live and Invest Overseas* magazine has named the Algarve coast the world's best place to retire overseas. The take-your-breath-away views, the constant sunshine, the near-perfect weather year-round, the food and wine, and the cost of a very rentable home or condo is irresistibly discounted, especially with a strong US dollar.
2. **El Poblado, Medellín, Colombia.** Offers a comfortable, tranquil, and

idyllic way of life for an affordable cost and is a top choice for city living on a budget.

3. **Las Terrenas, Dominican Republic.** Quintessential Caribbean with a French twist. A white-sand beach town with great restaurants. Establishing residency is easy, and the cost of living is one of the great bargains in today's Caribbean.

4. **Santa Familia, Cayo, Belize.** Life in Cayo is back-to-basics simple and sweet.

5. **Pau, France.** Known for its high quality of life, excellent health care, rich food, and cutting-edge art and fashion, France, for many people, is the definition of the good life, and the charms and appeals of French country life are unrivaled. Pau is known as the "Garden City."

6. **Chiang Mai, Thailand.** A low cost of living, great weather, rich history, and distinct culture entices many expats to live here.

7. **Playa del Carmen, Mexico.** Playa del Carmen is a little beach town that sits about an hour south of Cancún on Mexico's Riviera Maya.

8. **Barcelona, Spain.** On the Medi-

terranean Sea, this city is a vibrant, colorful, proud place. Its strong energy has not been dampened by Spain's ongoing economic woes.

9. **Granada, Nicaragua.** Nicaragua is a beautiful country, with a troubled history, that appeals to the romantic, poet, eco-traveler, surfer, and bargain hunter. The cost of living and of real estate makes it a steal. Geographically, Nicaragua is blessed with two long coastlines and two big lakes, plus volcanoes, highlands, rain forests, and rivers. This city is attracting expats in record numbers.

10. **Kota Kinabalu, Sabah, Malaysia.** This laid-back and quiet city is one of the most pleasant places to live in Asia and is incredibly welcoming. Its biggest practical advantages are a low cost of living and high standard (and low cost) of health care. You'd fill your days snorkeling, diving, boating, and ferry hopping from the city center to neighboring islands. This is a little-known, low-key, and low-population destination offering a tranquil, serene, and close-to-nature

lifestyle at a cost that's a global bargain.

Kiplinger says that people who want to live overseas but need to earn money have to be creative. Retired dentists and physicians sometimes open practices in their new locales. Some people are able to telecommute or consult for their former US-based employers, with nothing more than a laptop and an Internet connection. Financial advisers and accountants can create businesses helping other expats organize their financial lives. Retirees often find jobs teaching English, working at hotels, and giving tours to English-speaking travelers.

If you go online to Amazon or Barnes & Noble and search for "retire abroad," you'll find a lot of books on this subject. You want to read the most current ones about the location that interests you. *Never move to a fantasy place you haven't visited a lot.* The only person who has to like the place is you, but taxes, health care, and being far from family are all considerations to think hard about.

Lynn had visited Mexico during every vacation for the last twelve years. She even took an extended trip for six weeks to decide if she and her partner really wanted to move and build a retirement home there. After lots of investigation and research, they decided it was the right move for them, so in their fifties they quit their jobs. During the first year they rented and looked for land. They ended up buying a dilapidated home in a good area, on a nice piece of land. They hired a contractor and after numerous headaches and two more contractors, built the new, small home they now enjoy. They love the people. Both ladies speak Spanish, and the great weather and low cost of living make Mexico their retirement paradise. "This was a long-term dream with a lot of planning to it. Building involves a lot of headaches, but now we have the ideal home for us," Lynn notes.

Many boomers will travel on cruises and special trips throughout the United States, Europe, and Asia. But if living abroad is your dream, do lots of research, and investigate the area and costs. Jobs can be found, if having one makes the difference between living the dream or not. For some boomers, this is retirement nirvana.

VOLUNTEERING ABROAD

There are plenty of opportunities for seniors to volunteer abroad (and also domestically) after retirement. Senior volunteers can be found in the Peace Corps, working with religious organizations, and in diverse charity projects around the world.

Volunteer programs tend to be very flexible: seniors can commit to as little as a couple of weeks or as long as a couple of years. Investigate the opportunity and be sure both that it's a place you want to go to and that you have the skills they need. Many organizations have a program administration fee, and you are often responsible for your own travel expenses. There are lots of ways to see the world, from working with Mercy Ships in Africa to being a caretaker to actually moving to a new country like Terry did in Panama.

RESOURCES

Always check my website for up-to-date listings of terrific resources. Things can change quickly, especially in the travel area. Go to www.MyRetirementReinvention.com/resources.

CHAPTER 11
LEARN! EDUCATION AND NEW SKILLS (CHEAP OR FREE)

Pursue the things that engage you!

Many boomers want to continue to learn and are excited to take college classes in subjects that interest them. Some new activities require different skills, so many retirees will return to college to take courses that will enable them to pursue a dream or hobby. What about you?

What would you like to learn?

_____

_____

_____

_____

I spoke to the registrar's office at the University of Washington about the Access Program, which allows Washington State residents age sixty and older to audit one or two university courses per quarter on a space-available basis. The program is a great opportunity to take advantage of the extraordinary resources the campus has to offer, including outstanding faculty and a diverse student population.

Access students audit classes as nonmatriculated students. As an auditor, you may not participate in class discussions, take tests, or submit papers. As an Access student, you may enroll for a maximum of two courses per quarter for the low registration fee of five dollars. According to the gentleman from the registrar's office, hundreds of seniors take advantage of these course offerings every quarter.

My son, Jack, attends this large state university. One day I mentioned to his dad that people over sixty can take free classes at the university. My son quickly added, "The first row of my Intro to Architecture course is full of those people. And we have a few in my large philosophy class too." It seems some retirees already know about this bargain.

An amazing array of courses are available to audit. A small sample includes courses in the following:

Afro American studies
Archaeology
Art history
Astronomy
Business
China studies
Comparative literature, cinema, and media
Computer science
Dance
Design
Engineering
European studies
Foreign languages — dozens are offered
Genetics
History
International studies
Literature
Music
Psychology
Public health
Sociology
Various sciences
Women's studies

My home state isn't the only one doing this. Most public state universities and community colleges have free or nearly free programs that allow seniors to take college courses. Because these offerings can change and can vary by age and options offered, always check with the college registrar's office about the options available to attend that college for little or no charge.

The very popular website the Penny Hoarder (www.thepennyhoarder.com) pointed out some real bargains for free classes in almost every state nationwide. Here's a sample:

■ **California State University** waives all tuition and dramatically reduces campus fees for residents age sixty or older.

■ **Colorado:** Students age fifty-five and older may attend class on a space-available basis at Colorado State University. There is no tuition fee, but visitors don't get credit for attending class. At University of Colorado Denver, persons age sixty and above may enroll on a no-credit basis to attend classes as auditors when space is available.

■ **Connecticut:** Residents sixty-two and up may attend state colleges, including community colleges, for free.

■ The **Florida** college system (University of Florida, Florida State and branches) waives application, tuition, and student fees for those age sixty and above, but colleges will award no credit and will grant admission on a space-available basis.

■ **Illinois:** Upon admission, any senior citizen age sixty-five and up can attend regular credit courses at Illinois public institutions for free.

■ Any student in the **University of Maryland** system who's retired and over the age of sixty may have tuition waived, even for degree-granting programs.

■ At the **University of Minnesota,** seniors pay a ten-dollar fee per credit, but can audit for free.

■ The **University of Nevada, Las Vegas,** allows seniors sixty-two and up to take fall and spring courses free of charge.

■ **Ohio** residents at least sixty years old may attend class at any state college for free.

■ **Texas** law allows students sixty-five and up the opportunity to take six credit hours of undergraduate or graduate courses for free at public universities. *You are able to earn a degree at these institutions.*

■ **Wisconsin:** Adults sixty and up may audit classes at any University of Wisconsin campus for free, where space is available.

Don't expect to see any advertisements about these tuition-waived programs. The universities themselves do very little to publicize them. But just about every state's public colleges offer some kind of program for seniors to take classes. A few states allow you to earn college degrees at no charge except fees. No comprehensive list exists, but I try very hard to keep our resource listings on cost-free college classes up to date. Go to www.MyRetirementReinvention.com/resources.

Another option is Osher Lifelong Learning Institutes (www.osherfoundations.org). These institutes are partners with more than 120 lifelong learning programs on university and college campuses across the nation. The classes are of minimal cost and designed for older adults interested in learning for the joy of learning — without examinations or grading — and keeping in touch with a larger world. Some of the participating colleges and universities are Auburn University, Carnegie Mellon, Clemson University, Boise State University, Temple University, Iowa State University, and University of

California, Berkeley, to name a few. There is at least one affiliated school in every state. The number of courses available each term is limited.

WHAT ELSE CAN YOU LEARN?

"Between my demanding HR-recruiting job and raising my family, I never had a lot of time to do much else," notes Maggie, a smiling lady in her midsixties. "So when it came time to retire, I had a good plan for what I was going to do. I would become a seasoned and terrific chef." Not the kind who works in a restaurant, she emphasizes, but a terrific cook who could make delicious meals.

Maggie took a lot of cooking classes offered at different restaurants, catering companies, and cooking stores. She even tried the classes at Whole Foods. With each class, she improved her knowledge and ability to cook. "An added plus was you always got to eat whatever we made, so that helped me understand more about spices and what I liked and didn't. After a few months I started to select classes that offered world cultures and specific cuisines such as French or Italian or Thai. My family is amazed at how fabulously I cook now. They all laugh that when I was working it was microwave meals, whatever was quick or takeout," she says. Over the next few months, Maggie plans to master desserts. "I have a big sweet tooth," she laughs, "so I saved the best classes for last."

Cake decorating, flower arranging, photography, jewelry making, growing tomatoes, cooking, candle making, how to play a musical instrument — you can learn any kind of craft you can imagine.

The number one place to start is YouTube. Go there and search out your subject. There are hundreds (sometimes thousands) of free instructional videos. The great thing is that they show you exactly how to do whatever you might want to learn. I would pick the videos with lots of views. They usually are excellent. Many of the cooking classes were taught by chefs.

How-to courses are offered at community colleges, in colleges' continuing education departments, at senior centers, craft stores, fabric shops, yarn stores, quilt shops, and home-improvement stores like Home Depot or Lowe's.

Cooking classes are often taught at restaurants, high-end grocery stores, community centers, and in continuing education programs.

Go to Groupon for dance, cooking, glassblowing, and a multitude of fun things to do at a big discount.

ONE DAY UNIVERSITY

"I spent one day on the university's campus and enjoyed some lectures from some of America's top professors," says Leslie, who is a retired engineer. "I went and heard about 'Four Trials that Changed America'; 'Men, Women, and Politics'; and another course on 'The Three Greatest Films in American Cinema.' Each one was so interesting. The instructors were extraordinary. I loved it and I'll definitely go again."

When asked who was attending these classes, Leslie replied, "Mostly people in their sixties, definitely retired folks." Makes sense since the program she attended was sponsored by AARP.

One Day University (www.onedayu.com) was founded by Steven Schragis in 2006. He came up with the idea after he dropped his daughter at college in upstate New York to start her freshman year. The school had about a dozen professors spread around campus giving short talks about a variety of subjects. All the parents had a great time and had the same reaction: "I wish I were the one going to college!"

One Day U contracts with some of the

country's most wildly popular professors. They have won countless teaching awards and earned the highest possible ratings from their students on campus. Now they travel across the country with One Day University to educate and entertain students of all ages. You might hear a professor from Stanford, or UT Austin, or Yale. They really do select the professors that undergraduate students love best. Offered in more than forty-five cities across the country, these thought-provoking talks are also captured on video so you can "see" one even if you can't get to it live. "These are not free, but definitely worth the price of admission," Leslie says about the program she attended.

There are many options for you to take classes and learn something new. Check with your local librarian, as she may be aware of options where you reside. Ask in a favorite store if they offer courses. Lots of craft stores, like Michaels and Hobby Lobby, do.

RESOURCES

Go to www.MyRetirementReinvention.com/resources.

CHAPTER 12
START A BUSINESS

You are responsible for
the life you create.

As is probably clear by now, retirement doesn't necessarily mean stopping work. Indeed, a significant number of people want to own their own business. It may be a part-time thing or a full-time adventure, but it's a key part of their Retirement Reinvention plan. Some people pursue a hobby and turn it into a moneymaking venture. That said, running a small business can be very time-consuming, and starting from scratch has a high failure rate, especially if one expects the business to be a big source of income.

How can you own something but minimize your financial risk? A small business can also absorb all your time. How do you keep that in check? Most of the people I interviewed run their businesses part-time. And a lot of those businesses grew from a hobby or interest. There are people who have bigger dreams and want to run a business that will become highly profitable. That starts to sound a lot like a demanding real job. So if you are thinking about doing your own thing, read on.

Bobby grew up in a home with a lot of kids and had to learn to cook at a young age. He had no interest in dinner, but he had a lot of interest in baking cakes, cookies, and pies. He was the one to make the things for bake sales and the charity auctions for the sports team or any cause that needed a dessert to raffle off. He left that all behind when he started his professional life. During his very busy career as an estimator for a construction company, which required a lot of overtime, baking fell by the wayside. He just didn't do it anymore — that is, until he retired. Once Bobby had time on his hands, he decided to see if he could still master the oven.

He tried a few recipes. One Saturday, he made some desserts and invited a few neighbors over because his wife said they would get fat if they ate everything he made. The desserts were a big hit.

"At first people asked for my recipes," Bobby explains, "but I said no, they were family secrets. Then a few of the neighbors offered to buy desserts. And so, slowly but surely, people started ordering from me." Just by word of mouth (and some help from pictures of the desserts on Facebook), Bobby started a small business.

"You're not going to get rich baking like I do, but it sure is fun," he says. "I charge enough to cover the ingredients and make a little extra for my efforts. I spend a lot of time watching cooking shows, especially the dessert ones. I get ideas and certainly inspiration. If you enjoy baking, there's big business in making desserts, especially around holidays and for party times like graduations, birthdays, anniversaries, etc. My favorite thing is to make pies, but I do a really good job on cakes, so they are very popular. Who would have thought I'd be a chef in retirement? Not me, that's for sure. Going back to a hobby I loved from childhood has made my retirement interesting and fun."

Many people venture into a small cooking business. Brownies, cookies, and cakes are all in high demand. One lady specializes in wedding cakes. She mastered frosting designs and has her signature creations.

Gail and her husband ran a real estate business for more than two decades. In her late fifties, Gail began to feel drained by the demands of the business, and it was apparent to me that she was burned out and really done with her career. The couple had a Florida condo, and Gail wanted to spend four to five months of the year there, which meant selling the business.

Gail took a year off after the sale, but within months, feeling bored and unmoored, she called me to discuss her Retirement Reinvention options. The couple had moved to be near their daughter; it was only a hundred miles away from their former home, but it meant leaving the town they had worked in for decades. As we discussed her interests, Gail told me about some all-natural products from Young Living. She used its supplements, oils, and cleaning products. She liked them so much she had persuaded all her friends to use them too.

This turned out to be an opportunity. "It's a multilevel marketing organization. I join and get a discount on the products I personally buy and use, plus I earn a bit of income on any products my friends buy from me," she explained. Gail was dead set against starting another large-scale business. She was pleased that she could make selling these products into a part-time, flexible activity. She found out the company had a great training program on how to use their oils for better health. She took these classes, which then allowed her to educate people she met. She would be able to teach workshops too. Within a year, she was earning several hundred dollars a month. She worked only as much as she wanted, saying, "It's not really a job. I love how I feel connected to the company and the education I'm getting. I enjoy teaching others about these great products. They are good for the individual. The cleaning products work and are environmentally safe. Being a snowbird, all I need is myself and an Internet connection to run this little business. It's an ideal retirement job for me." And she's in a hot area — essential oils top many of the multi-level marketing (MLM) lists as a top sales product.

MLM opportunities abound. There is everything from Jeunesse, which rids people of wrinkles, to Amway, Pampered Chef, and Scentsy, which sells scented candles, to Mary Kay and Avon, and Cabi clothing sold in your home.

Now, should you run out and join one of these companies? That depends on your goals. If you want to make a few bucks and can recover your investment fairly easily, then maybe this is a good idea. Overall, MLM has worked for some people, but it hasn't always worked out well for most.

These marketing companies may have a decent product and be full of good intentions, but the industry has flaws. You need to do research and really *look* under the hood before you lay your money down. Stay clear of companies that promise big fortunes to be made by sales from new recruits instead of outside customers. This tactic has gotten a lot of these companies in hot water with the government. Your job, they say, is to "run an empire" and have lots of people selling underneath you. The bottom line is this: someone has to sell the products or no one makes money.

There are success stories, though. Lori was the manager of a hair salon with six stylists. She handled the accounting, inventory, payroll, plus answered the phones and checked people in. "One day a rep came in and asked why we weren't selling skin-care products," Lori says. She gave Lori some samples, which is how Lori discovered Rodan + Fields. After attending an educational event, Lori went and signed up to become a Rodan + Fields consultant at age fifty-seven (lorih.myrandf.com). She developed this business into a nice part-time venture.

Fast-forward four years, and the salon Lori worked at lost its lease and closed down. At sixty-two, Lori now has a very established business with a multilevel marketing system. That means she not only sells the products but also signs up new consultants to work under her guidance. For Lori this is a part-time thing. "It's all your own, so you can make it what you want," she says. "I work about five to ten hours a week, earning hundreds of dollars a month. I love meeting so many new people, and this skin-care line is truly wonderful. I can control my time, so I can be a very active grandmother too."

Lori recruits people into this business model. "This is a great opportunity for retired individuals to meet people, have fun, attend conventions, and make some extra money," she says. "That, to me, is the perfect way to be actively retired." Lori says most sales come from connecting to people and getting referrals.

And she says she chose this skin-care line because of the doctors' reputation and how they built an eight-billion-dollar company selling Proactive. "I stayed with this organization because after I used the products, my skin looked terrific. I am selling something that works, which is essential for me to do this," she notes.

Multilevel marketing opportunities

abound. Some sage, cautious advice:

- Love the product and what it does — whether nutrition/supplements, skin care, makeup, fitness, etc.
- Be sure the company has great products.
- Research the company and what it stands for.
- Research its reputation.
- Examine the compensation plan: the costs of supplies and how much is paid.
- Do you need to stock inventory? (Keep in mind that this is a deficit.)
- How much does the website cost you to run?
- Any minimum amount of products you have to buy per month?
- Does the company provide leads?
- Must you find all the new customers yourself?

Look at the start-up costs, ongoing expenses, and taxes that must be subtracted from the profit. Then decide if this is the right retirement venture for you.

IF YOU CREATE IT, YOU CAN SELL IT

A jolly lady with a big smile, Barb worked in technology sales. When she got laid off, she came to me for career counseling. She had grown to hate how male-dominated the industry was. She worried that it would be very hard to find a permanent job because she was fifty-six and her last two positions were as a contractor. It seemed to me that this career might be done for her. She was burned-out and needed to consider a different option. She could retire, as her husband had an excellent paying position. When we discussed her interests, one stood out — painting. She loved it and painted in her free time. This creative hobby would be the basis of her new business. We discussed how she could paint landscapes and flowers that would appeal to consumers. Then we talked about community festivals where she could show her work and sell it. Most of the festivals required an entrance fee, so she did a lot of research and entered a couple, to try it out. She sold several paintings and even got a couple of custom orders. Several months later, she launched a website for her business, Create Your Wow (www.createyour wow.com), and started a Facebook page for her customers and those interested in other festivals at which she'd be showing. Barb now paints in her free time and books only the festivals she wants. November and December and summer are the prime months. She is getting a better idea of what is commercial and sells. To fill the slower period, she teaches art classes at YMCA and senior centers. Barb is very happy and says her retirement is so much fun she wishes she'd retired sooner. And the business is profitable — something she wasn't sure would happen. Yet it did.

ACTION STEP

Before you start any business, have a conversation with an accountant or tax preparer. A small business may require you to pay taxes, depending on how much you earn, and you can also deduct the cost of supplies, advertising, business travel, and other valid business expenses. Best to get some professional guidance earlier rather than later!

THE MAGICAL WORLD OF TIDYING UP

Some people just love to be organized, but many are at a loss for how to do just that. Mary had retired and was decompressing from her high-stress management position when she got a call from her close friend,

Beth, saying she needed help. Beth and her husband had decided to downsize. Easier said than done, because Beth's closets and attic were overflowing with stuff, and so was her garage. To fit into a much smaller house, this couple had to get rid of a lot of things. Beth felt so overwhelmed she didn't know where to start.

Mary came over and for the next few weeks worked with Beth and her husband to streamline their possessions and start taking things out of the house. Some things went to a garage sale (and they did have a big one), larger furniture went for sale on Craigslist, some things went to the local Goodwill store, and other stuff ended up in the dump. They moved, and the couple insisted they had parted with as much as they could. Beth also wanted some help organizing the new house, to be certain that she didn't overstuff it. So Mary went along to make sure everything was in its place and to help consolidate things. More and more "stuff" got edited out. When the project was finally done, Mary realized that, for her, it had been nothing but fun. She loved organizing other people's possessions, and she felt she'd really helped out her friend. She recognized that her friends weren't the only people downsizing.

For a lot of baby boomers, parting with "stuff" is challenging and kind of sad. Mary realized that she could be kind but resourceful and helpful. Her new business, Less Is Better, was born. It didn't take very long for her to find a lot of clients interested in her service. She charges a reasonable hourly rate, and if she helps with a garage sale, she gets part of the profits. If she does the garage sale completely by herself, she gets 80% of the profits. To find clients, Mary made some inexpensive business cards and started telling people what she was doing. She posted a short description on the neighborhood Facebook page, which brought in some new business. She contacted real estate agents, because they would know people who were selling and needed to move. She also contacted people in the moving business and made sure that they had her cards too. Mary schedules her business, so she can take on a project if she wants to, or if she has something else she's planning to do, she can turn that particular client down. It's been a very rewarding job for her because she enjoys organizing people and knows she is helping them too.

Mary did three very smart things to get her business flourishing. She:

- made inexpensive business cards
- posted a short description on the neighborhood Facebook page
- networked and contacted real estate agents and people in the moving business to get referrals

Rebecca Crichton, executive director of the Northwest Center for Creative Aging, says, "Downsizing homes is going to be a big business as baby boomers age and move. Most boomers confess that they simply have too much stuff to go from a big house to a smaller house without doing a thorough streamlining and giving away or selling a lot of stuff. I can easily predict that there's going to be a lot of need for people who are good organizers to help baby boomers and elderly people downsize."

Rebecca says that getting rid of stuff you no longer want or can keep is a more difficult process than you'd think.

"People often feel some sort of shame about owning or having too much stuff," she explains. "They feel like something is wrong with them for wanting to keep stuff. Some think it's too big a task and that they can't decide what to part with. People feel guilty about giving away things they received as gifts from others even though they have no need for them anymore.

"Men and women both suffer from a hoarding phenomenon where it is difficult to let go. There may be shame in having stuff, and there may also be shame in not being able to let it go. It's not the stuff," says Rebecca. "It's the memories that are really the issue. The kids' things from childhood, the family days gone by. They see these memories in the things they hang on to. They represent being a good mom or dad. These things represent the past. In fact, looking at the stuff is really a reminder of times that are now over, and maybe some grief work needs to happen."

One thing many people hoard is photos. A lot of boomers have pictures in boxes — and boxes — in their homes. Yes, those printed pictures date from long before digital became the rage. Offering a service to scan and organize photos, and/or convert old format movies to digital files might be a much-needed part-time business. You would have to invest in a fast, high-quality scanner, but you could quickly pay for it by charging to scan those boxes of old photos. This is a portable business too. Some stores charge for this, but you could go to the person's residence and do the work there.

Marilyn is a retired hospital nurse who winters in Saint Petersburg, Florida. To relax from her stressful job, she would sew. She'd alter her own clothes, and her husband's and daughters'. Having also made clothes for her daughters and herself, she'd become an accomplished seamstress. It was a nice hobby. After she took the hospital's retirement offer, she had a lot of time on her hands. Both daughters were off in college. She and her husband bought the Florida condo in the first winter of her retirement. Not knowing anyone, Marilyn thought about taking in some sewing to keep her busy at night. She went to a morning coffee in her development, where more than two hundred people socialize and catch up on the weekly news. When she introduced herself to the room, she mentioned that she did alterations. Once the intros were done, she was swamped by a dozen ladies wanting to hire her to do clothing alterations for them. This is how she launched a part-time business in her snowbird home. All her business comes from word of mouth. "The nice thing," Marilyn says, "is this job is very portable. I simply bring my sewing machine with me, and my supplies, and I'm in business. I do this now at home too. It's easy, and I only accept work I want to do. It's nice, easy work and I enjoy being busy. Plus, making some extra money is helpful too."

IT MAY TAKE TIME TO
LAUNCH YOUR NEXT PHASE

A very personable and outgoing man, white-haired Sandy was a sales and marketing executive. He traveled a lot and had a demanding job. He was sixty-five when he retired. During his working life, Sandy had no time to pursue his passion for photography. So he took the first two years of retirement to study everything he could find out about photography — camera usage, lenses, and how exactly to take better photographs.

Sandy realized he was lonely without any work colleagues and decided to teach a class for a local parks and recreation organization. Three people came. Not an encouraging start, but Sandy put some serious brainpower into considering how he could launch classes teaching other camera lovers. He defined his business model saying, "I'm a better teacher than I am a pro photographer." He named his new venture SnapShot Sandy. After some extensive market research, he decided to try offering a Groupon class, How to Take Better Digital

Photographs, for twenty-nine dollars. The course drew some interest and he reoffered the Groupon. He taught small groups from his own home. This is where he and I met. I was a student, and as Sandy gradually offered advanced courses, I took them all. I even did some private one-on-one coaching sessions with Sandy and have a beautiful landscape scene hanging in our family room that I took with Sandy's assistance.

To date, Sandy has taught more than twenty-six hundred students, many he now considers his friends. Word of mouth and repeat clients fill his classes today. The flexibility of offering classes on his own schedule was essential since Sandy spends eight to nine months a year in Arizona for health reasons. In Arizona he approached offering classes differently. There he got hired on by the parks district and offers numerous classes for them. They do the marketing, and he's paid a flat fee for each course taught. He also teaches classes at Luke Air Force Base for active military, family members, and veterans. He does not charge them any money to attend; this is his way of giving back.

Sandy advises others, "In retirement you should do something flexible that is fun. My little company keeps me busy, and I make enough to cover my habit, as buying new cameras, and more or better lenses, is quite expensive. For me, it is the enjoyment factor and that this business allows me to meet so many nice people who love my hobby too."

HOW WE LOVE OUR PETS

Retired from a successful career in advertising, Suzi West knew that as a lady in her late fifties she still needed to have social interaction and wanted to make a new career for herself that was doing something fun but meaningful.

Suzi had always volunteered in animal shelters. "One year before I retired, I got this idea to do dog parties. I knew I could try to make this work here in Southern California. My goal is to make the parties interactive between the animals and their owners," says Suzi.

Voilà — she started Party Animals (www.padogpartyplanner.com), a service company that offers parties for dogs and pet-walking services. But it was the originality of dog parties that caught the eye of customers.

The results have been amazing — dog lovers think this is so original, and it's a fantastic way to get dogs and owners together.

"For me," says Suzi, "I'm doing this solely because I have passion for the dogs. It was never about the money."

To fill in the downtime, she does doggie playdates and also dog walking. Suzi says, "I'm happier than I could ever dream possible. This business gives me something important to do that touches my heart. I'm a go-getter type of person, and I can't just sit on my rump and play mahjong all day. I'm 100% glad I'm doing this. I have no intention of stopping. It really satisfies my need to be helpful to the animals and the owners. I get to do something I really love." Now that's what retirement should really be about!

READY FOR A BIG BIZ?

Franchises are everywhere. You know the big ones: McDonald's, Subway, Burger King, 7-Eleven, Domino's, to name a few. Most of these can have huge start-up costs, since they require a great (and often expensive) location plus a brick-and-mortar facility with equipment and buildouts and employees. That doesn't mean you should write off franchises. In fact, for the right person they can offer the perfect profitable solution to owning your own business.

Diane Pleuss runs FranChoice (www.fran choice.com), which offers free services to individuals considering a franchise business. This service (paid for by the franchise companies) offers coaching and evaluation to see if you would make a good franchise owner. If it concludes this might be right for you, the next step is to identify what type of business. It also helps with that.

Diane and I discussed franchises as an option for retirees.

"The best candidate has a true passion to be a business owner," she said. "He or she has that fire in their belly, has been previously successful, and is coachable but not necessarily a big risk taker."

Does that describe you? Do you want a proven business model and established infrastructure? Would you value the comprehensive marketing plan and training that a successful franchise offers? This path to creating a new large-scale business is really a bridge career, as this is going to be a full-time job for most people.

Who is the typical person attracted to do this once they "retire"?

Diane said, "Most of the clients I work with are trying to replace their salary with this new business. That usually means profits over $100,000 a year. The ideal candidate typically has good business skills and has been successful in the past. Drawing on those transferable skills (meaning they can move from one job to another), the franchiser's training helps them get off to a solid start." The key here is that this business will be your own. You can make it as big as you want. Since most people are trying to replace their day-job salary, once they start earning that kind of profit they often look to hire a manager so they can have more time of their own. Others grow the business into multiple franchises and continue to manage them all. There are a lot of options and they all depend on your goals and what you personally want.

This franchise option that most pre-retirees and new retirees gravitate toward is a service-based business. This can be defined as the following:

- A business that cannot be offshored
- One with product not made in China
- One not impacted by the Internet or Amazon
- One you want to run out of an office suite or your home

An example would be a senior-care business, which requires an investment between $75,000 and $150,000. The business owner is in charge of hiring caregivers and providing them with seniors who live at home and need help to remain there. The business owner will grow the business by securing referral sources and eventually have somewhere between sixty and one hundred caregivers. This business model requires excellent scheduling, recruiting, interviewing, hiring, and business-management skills.

These kinds of service-based businesses cost money to launch. The typical investment, according to Diane, is between $75,000 and $200,000. This money covers the franchise fees, operation costs, any needed locations or buildings, rental fees, equipment, etc. Typical investment is $120,000.

You're probably thinking, *How do I come up with that kind of money?* Some people use their severance or an inheritance, but this is where a franchise consultant like Diane is helpful. One thing she brought to my attention was that you can use your 401(k) as a direct investment. Currently, as I write this, if you roll over your 401(k) to open a new business, you don't have to pay any tax penalties.

You might assume that the bigger the

franchise cost, the better and more profitable it will be. "Not true," says Diane. "There is no direct correlation between the investment level and what you can make."

What kinds of service-based business are we talking about? Some of the most profitable, as noted by *Entrepreneur* magazine, are:

- Bookkeeping, accounting, and payroll services
- Residential and commercial cleaning
- Automotive equipment rental and leasing
- Medical claims billing services
- Handyman services
- Pet services: grooming, walking, pet-sitting
- Editorial services: proofreading, editing, ghostwriting, book doctoring, webpage content provider, magazine/newsletter article writing
- Repair service: computers, lawn mowers, snowblowers, appliances, small engines, etc.

The attractive factor in a service-based organization is that you get repeat business. This provides a good cash flow. The owner needs to be able to market, of course, particularly in their community, to help build the business.

Here's my advice: Think *long and hard* before you make a major investment. *Not all franchises are created equal.* Do your homework and research before you invest any money in any kind of franchise. Talk to people who actually have that business and are operating it, to learn about the pros and the cons. What did they find most effective in building the business and marketing to get new customers? What challenges do they face? What kind of profit is reasonable to expect?

Diane's advice is that your passion is for being a *business owner,* not being, say, a "cleaning freak." She offers questionnaires and a comprehensive consultation to help match a person to a business, based on the individual's goals, skills, and interests. More men choose this path. A few couples try to build a business and even hire their adult children so they can leave the business to them. I asked Diane what was new and hot. Apparently eyelash extension is catching on because it's a repeatable service business and all you need is a business suite. You divide it so you have practitioners doing the work while you run the business. Customers need to rebook every three or four weeks. The key to success is having a service business that's repeatable, with the same customers coming back frequently for that service.

Victoria Marshall owned a tour-map-publishing business where she oversaw fifteen employees and had franchises too. Finding it demanding and stressful, she sold it at age fifty-five. Her husband was an engineer with a lot of outdoor hobbies, and he was happy with retired life. As Victoria recovered from the stressful way she had been living, she realized she did not enjoy retirement as much as she thought she would.

Together the couple purchased an existing publication, *Senior Guidebook,* to leverage the mailing lists and advertisers. Along with giving it a new title, they freshened its design and writing, expanded its editorial scope, and broadened the magazine's appeal. Victoria says, "My husband and I are boomers with parents in their eighties — one with dementia. We face important questions and challenges that are shared by thousands of other boomers. That's what is covered in this Northwest magazine."

They cover how to age well, how to help parents make tough decisions and transitions, and how to live fulfilling lives as older adults. They seek local resources and advice, all of which make their new publication, called *3rd Act Magazine,* a timely and important resource for readers. (Sign up for a copy at www.3rdactmagazine.com.)

The magazine is currently published quarterly in the Northwest, with articles and stories that speak directly to boomers and older adults. The writers and contributors are experts and progressive thinkers in all matters related to navigating this stage of life. One of the covers for a winter issue shows three vibrant-looking skiers with big smiles on their faces. They look so young and engaging. Victoria revealed their ages, which surprised me: seventy-five, seventy-two, and fifty-nine. They looked young and energized. The article says, "Snowbirds — some fly north."

The couple's goal was to create a vital magazine. It is, with its vibrant colors and engaging and informative ideas.

In her Retirement Reinvention job, Victoria handles content development and advertising, and her husband handles operations. They have no staff now and can't pass off the minutiae anymore — they have to do that too. When asked about undertaking this big entrepreneurial venture at age sixty, Victoria offered some wise guidance:

"Opening any business is not without risk. It makes your lifestyle much less flexible, as you have new obligations and commitments. Running any business takes sacrifice. Be as realistic as you can be about the true cost of the financial and time investment. Then know it will take *more money* and *more time* than you planned on." Victoria also raised some serious cautions: "Ask yourself how much money you can afford to *lose* on this investment of starting a new business. It's very hard at this age to make up for having spent your entire 401(k) to get the business off the ground, only to find it fails. So don't plan on spending any more than what you *can comfortably lose* without destroying your financial future. Be careful," she emphasized. "It may look great on paper, but it will be harder than it seems. If you lose this investment, it's very difficult at this age to recoup that income."

Where did the money come from to start *3rd Act Magazine?* Victoria and her husband went to the Small Business Administration (SBA) with the business proposal and plan. It was heavily scrutinized before they gave them the start-up loan. Many people aren't aware that the SBA makes loans to older people. Your plan needs to be solid, and if the SBA turns you down for a loan, Victoria pointed out, "That's *real* feedback, so pay attention. Do you really still want to take the risk? I say no, but you are the only one who can answer that question." Sage advice. If you want to look into an SBA loan, visit a local bank or lending institution that participates in SBA programs. Find more info at www.sba.gov.

WHO IS DOING THIS?

Business Insider recently revealed that in the past ten years baby boomers between ages fifty-five and sixty-four have the highest rate of entrepreneurial activity in the United States. It is predominantly men who are opening new businesses. They are well educated and work alone or with their spouse. They keep it small, fewer than five employees. And they are often pursuing hobbies and have a strong personal network.

Most people know that Colonel Sanders started Kentucky Fried Chicken at age sixty-five. *Forbes* recently ran an article about why so many people over age fifty-five were turning to entrepreneurship. The reasons included the following:

- They are attracted by the opportunity to create a business that is responsive to their unique needs, interests, and desires.

- According to an AARP survey, almost 80% of people over fifty-five want to continue working, more than half in part-time work.
- Baby boomers have many years of experience, expertise, seasoned judgment, and proven performance to support creating a new business.
- Many people over fifty-five have developed excellent contacts in the business world that can facilitate their new business venture.
- They have accumulated funds to support starting a new business.

Want some outside advice for free? Contact SCORE (www.score.org), a branch of the Small Business Administration that provides free advice for potential organizations, start-ups, and existing businesses. They have helped nearly one million businesspeople. SCORE is run by volunteer businesspeople helping small-business people solve business problems. Volunteers give freely of their time, energy, and knowledge to help others. SCORE volunteers donate over one million hours each year to support colleagues working in their local communities.

Find more resources at www.MyRetirementReinvention.com/resources.

CHAPTER 13
LIVE A BETTER FUTURE

Amaze yourself. Just do it!

Retirement is not a vacation. To make yours successful, fun, and happy, you need to plan for it. The most important thing is to retire on your own terms and not be pushed into it. If you're in your fifties or sixties, you really need to have an exit strategy. Sooner or later, *you will retire.* Maybe it will be on your own terms — I sure hope that happens, but some people's employers will nudge them out. Having a plan and knowing you can decompress, make a transition, and develop a great life is your ace in the hole when the time comes.

How do you treat retirement like a career? Let's see what we can glean from what we have learned.

GOALS AND PURPOSE

You need reasons to get out of bed in the morning. Something that matters and has meaning. By now, you should have a clear idea of what that is. Maybe it's giving back and helping others. Maybe it's a part-time job living out a hobby you enjoy. Maybe it's starting a business. Whatever your choices are, you should set long- and short-term goals to keep life interesting. Pay attention to your bucket list, and be sure you are crossing off the items you really want to do.

SOCIAL CONNECTION

We all need friends and family around to encourage us in the trials and tribulations of life. In the office we have colleagues to collaborate with, and that's often the missing piece in a retiree's life.

It can be difficult to make new friends when you first retire. But by volunteering, taking classes, attending community events, exploring hobbies, or finding a part-time job, you can — and will — meet new people.

Retirement is a time to reconnect with old friends and classmates. Try Facebook. If you can't find someone, post a message on your Facebook page, because another acquaintance may have the contact info you need.

If you plan to move, consider how you will

make friends and engage in the new community. Check out organizations and clubs before you get there.

NEED SOME EXTRA CASH?

Look for a job doing something new and fun. Explore working in a hobby area you love. Most likely you'll want a part-time job. Ask neighbors and friends. They may know of something you'd enjoy. When seeking a part-time position, networking is critical. Many of these jobs aren't publicized.

CHANGE IS NEVER EASY

And retiring is a very *big* change. It can be a prime time of life if you make it about doing things that make you happy. That was my goal in writing this book — to provide ideas and direction for creating a more satisfying life.

If you read the book cover to cover, you discovered how dozens and dozens of baby boomers are making retirement the time of their life. I hope that you read about new ways you too might enjoy things and learned about many fun options you hadn't thought of before. You can use this book as a reference guide and simply read the chapters you are interested in.

Now, retirement will not be all fun and

games. You know life will intrude and hit you with losses — losing family, friends, and health as we age are the hardest things to deal with. But there can be a lot of joy in the 9,000 days you likely have ahead of you. Only you can make those days good ones. You are the driver of your life. Remember — you can be a joiner, a starter, or a failed retiree.

Let's finalize your retirement plan. Understand that this is a *flexible* and *adaptable* plan. You should review it annually on your birthday and make updates and changes. You need retirement goals, just like you needed them when you worked. These should be written down so you can review and update them. If you haven't retired yet, *use a pencil* to create your retirement plan. Erasers make it oh so easy to change. Or use an app or word processor — the point is to be flexible and make changes as new opportunities arise.

MY RETIREMENT PLAN

RESIDENCE(S)

I plan to live in (name city, state, and development if you know it; snowbirds list both):

1. _____BUY or RENT
2. _____BUY or RENT

HOW FAMILY WILL PLAY
INTO MY RETIREMENT

_____

_____

_____

_____

_____

RETIREMENT-REINVENTION WORK

I plan to volunteer, get a job, or start a business. My exact plan is:

_____

_____

_____

_____

_____

_____

Where will I make new friends?

_____

_____

_____

_____

_____

_____

How will I make a difference?

_____

_____

_____

_____

_____

BUDGET

To meet my monthly budget of $_____, I will need to earn $_____ per month and plan to get a paying job.

☐ *YES*   ☐ *NO*

My job will be doing _____

OBSTACLES TO OVERCOME

List the problems clearly.

_____

_____

_____

_____

_____

Write out solutions to the problems.

_____

_____

_____

_____

_____

EDUCATION

List classes and educational programs you want to experience or take.

_____

_____

_____

_____

_____

TRAVEL

List the places you want to see — and when you'll go there.

_____
_____
_____
_____
_____
_____

I MUST DO . . .

Name the two things that you really must do, because if you never did them you'd really regret it. Note the date when, or by which, they will happen. Keep in mind that your health and energy will fade as you age, so put these items high on your priority list.

1._____

2._____

MY BUCKET LIST

Bucket List (from chapter 2)
Here are the ten things I definitely want to do before I die:

1. _____

2. _____

3. _____

4. _____

5. _____

6. _____

7. _____

8. _____

9. _____

10. _____

The most important piece of retirement for me to be happy is:

_____

_____

_____

_____

CONCLUDING THOUGHTS

Be flexible! Your plan is just a plan. You can alter it, and you can add in new things as you test-drive them. You may meet new people who take you on new adventures. If you try something and it's not great for you, don't do it again. Make sure any volunteer work feels rewarding. Most of all, *enjoy* your days!

Nine thousand days are ahead and waiting for you to fill them doing things you love. May your days be filled with mostly sunny skies, fulfilling relationships, and a meaningful purpose to get up in the morning. Please, take a little bit of time to care for others. Being of service to others is renewing and rewarding in its own unique way, so do add that onto your to-do plan.

This is the prime time of your life, because it's the time you are alive right now, with so much ahead of you yet to be done. You have time to relax, to be peaceful, and also to add new people and activities. The life ahead is unwritten. You, and you alone, create it. So definitely enjoy yourself. Live it up. Try new things. Make new friends. Reconnect with some old ones. And help others whenever you can. That is the perfect retirement plan.

MORE CAREER HELP IS AVAILABLE

"Robin Ryan is America's top career counselor."
— *The Boston Globe*

CAREER-COUNSELING SERVICES
Robin assists individual clients worldwide, *anytime* and *anywhere,* with retirement planning, interviewing, résumé writing, career changing, job searches, and salary negotiations. For more info, go to www.RobinRyan.com, e-mail her at Robin@RobinRyan.com, or call her office at (425) 226-0414.

HAVE ROBIN SPEAK TO YOUR GROUP
Robin offers seminars, workshops, and webinars. She frequently speaks to corporate, association, and college alumni groups about careers and retirement. Learn more at www.careerspeakerusa.com or e-mail her at Robin@RobinRyan.com.

E-Newsletter

Featuring Robin's career advice column. Sign up free on her homepage at www.RobinRyan.com.

Books and Audio CDs

Robin's books are available online and in bookstores. These include:

60 Seconds & You're Hired!
Over 40 & You're Hired!
Soaring on Your Strengths
Winning Resumes (Second Edition)
Winning Cover Letters (Second Edition)
What to Do with the Rest of Your Life

Contact Robin Ryan at (425) 226-0414
E-mail her at Robin@RobinRyan.com
Visit her websites at
www.RobinRyan.com and
www.MyRetirementReinvention.com

ACKNOWLEDGMENTS

While writing this book, I met so many interesting people. And being over fifty-five myself, I found out about a lot of organizations I really wanted to get involved with.

A major, heartfelt thank-you goes out to all the clients and individuals who told me their retirement stories and allowed me to use them so you could learn from their experiences. Any mistakes that might have been made in the retelling are mine.

I appreciated the professionals who generously gave me a few hours of their time to help with background and to share their insights into the world of retirees.

Some individuals did a lot to support me, and they deserve a special mention. Thank you for your help and connections, Tracy White, Gail Pierepiekarz, and Henry Devries. Sarah Williams shared her editorial assistance on a piece that was close to my heart. She is the best editor I know, and I am grateful for her generous assistance. Sunny Murphy went above and beyond what any good friend might do. She gave me connections and read the entire book, offering insightful feedback. You are simply wonderful, Sunny. My brother Dave Christiano, who is a film producer and has written numerous screenplays, took time from his busy life and helped me improve the quality of my storytelling.

A special shout-out to my neighbor Sue Caile, who walked my doggies every day, so I could use that extra hour a day to write.

I have a wonderful team that is always there to support my work and assist in the things I do to help others in their career advancement and job search. Many thanks to Dee Murphy and Leslie Ault, who worked closely with me on this book and offered ways to improve it.

My two doggies came and sat by my feet as I wrote, offering support the best way they knew how to give. I could reach out and pet them or hold them as I worked on the pages of this book. Zoey and Duffy are true family members, and they add much joy to my life.

My family is my world. To my husband, Steve, and my son, Jack, big hugs and a mountain of gratitude for understanding when the house wasn't perfect, meals didn't get made, and laundry piled up, but you never complained as I kept on writing. I love you both more than anything else.

A special thank-you goes to my agent, Jane von Mehren, who provided terrific insight and editorial suggestions to make this book what it is today. You are terrific! The great people at Penguin, particularly my editor and champion, Patrick Nolan, and the extraordinary Matt Klise. Matt shared his editorial genius to help improve the final version of this book — I'm so lucky to have him on my team.

Finally, to you, my reader, thank you for purchasing this book. I spent two years of my life creating it so you could benefit. Do go to the resources pages, as I'm continually adding in new tools, articles, and insights to help you. If you find this book was helpful, connect with me by e-mailing me at Robin@RobinRyan.com.

ABOUT THE AUTHOR

Oprah, Dr. Phil, NBC Nightly News, Fox News, and CNN are only a few of the more than two thousand TV and radio shows where **Robin Ryan** has been seen offering her advice.

She is the bestselling author of *60 Seconds & You're Hired!, Over 40 & You're Hired!, Soaring on Your Strengths, Winning Resumes, Winning Cover Letters,* and *What to Do with the Rest of Your Life.*

Robin Ryan has been quoted or featured in most major magazines and newspapers, including *Businessweek, Money, Newsweek, Fortune, Good Housekeeping, Forbes, USA Today, The Wall Street Journal, The New York Times, The Seattle Times, Los Angeles Times,* and *Chicago Tribune.*

A career counselor for over twenty years, Robin Ryan uses her expertise daily in her consulting practice, where she helps individual clients land great jobs, get promotions, change careers, secure higher salaries, or plan for their Retirement Reinvention. A licensed vocational counselor, Robin offers telephone, Skype, and in-person consultations.

A highly sought-after corporate trainer and national speaker, she frequently appears at corporate training sessions, libraries, college alumni gatherings, and association conferences.

Robin Ryan holds a master's degree in counseling and education from Suffolk University and a bachelor's degree in sociology from Boston College. She is the former director of counseling services at the University of Washington.

Contact her at (425) 226-0414, e-mail Robin@RobinRyan.com, or visit her website at www.RobinRyan.com or www.MyRetire mentReinvention.com.

The employees of Thorndike Press hope you have enjoyed this Large Print book. All our Thorndike, Wheeler, and Kennebec Large Print titles are designed for easy reading, and all our books are made to last. Other Thorndike Press Large Print books are available at your library, through selected bookstores, or directly from us.

For information about titles, please call:
(800) 223-1244

or visit our website at:
gale.com/thorndike

To share your comments, please write:
Publisher
Thorndike Press
10 Water St., Suite 310
Waterville, ME 04901